Selling The Way America Buys

Dr. Franklin,

Thank you for keeping me healthy enough to write this.

You always bring your "A-Game"!

Sincerely,

Selling The Way America Buys

Steve Bryant

S.E.L.F. PUBLISHING
Simple, Effective, Literary Focusing on Publishing

Selling The Way America Buys

Book Cover Designed By K.T.H.S.R! Creative
Editor Marc Baldwin

Quantity purchasing for company promotions or educational needs, must be requested from the Promotional Department at:

S.E.L.F. PUBLISHING
4075 S. Durango Drive
Suite 111 #220
Las Vegas, NV 89147
Visit us at www.yourpublisher.org

All companies mentioned or profiled in this book were selected by the author solely for the purpose of illustration. The publisher disclaim any warranty, expressed or implied, regarding the recommendation or information contained in this book.

ISBN 09776335-4-3

Library of Congress Control Number 2006930995

Printed In The United States Of America

"This book is dedicated to my wife Rosanne and my dog Mandy, both of whom believed in me when no one else did. I love you both with all my heart."

CONTENTS

Introduction

While I love to read, especially sales books, I have always hated longwinded book introductions. Since I want you to have as much fun reading this as I did writing it, I'll keep this one short and to the point.

Sales skills are a part of everything we do. We're always selling something: a product, service, idea, or even ourselves. How well you can sell determines just how successful you'll be in any given endeavor. This book is full of a lifetime of stories and examples that will show you how to improve your performance in any selling situation.

I really want to thank you for buying this book. With all the great sales books on the market, I'm very flattered that you chose this one. I'm confident you'll find it fun, informative, and interesting. By using the ideas and tips presented here, you will be paying me the nicest compliment any author can ever have. I hope your life and career will be as rewarding as mine.

Good selling!

It's All Been Done Before, So Do It Better!

Find success and copy it! Change it to suit your purposes, add your own spin, and you'll succeed. Economic times are tough? It's not the first time. Find out what successful people did in previous depressed times and you're virtually assured of success. Economy booming? Again, it's not the first time. Study people who succeeded in prosperous times, and you can too. It's not rocket science!

We've all heard the quote of writer George Santayana, from his *Life of Reason, Reason in Common Sense,* "Those who cannot remember the past are condemned to repeat it." Still, few people take it to heart. Far too often, someone says, "I'd rather make my own mistakes." And they do, blissfully unaware that the solutions to their problems already exist.

Success is so close for most people, yet relatively few really find it.

A quick example from my days in advertising: Doug was a salesperson for a major telecommunications company in 1978 and was outselling his peers almost five to one. What was his secret? He learned what successful communications salespeople did during the early 1970's, a similar time of gas "shortages," a sluggish economy and rapid technological innovation.

None of his peers bothered to see the similarities in economic climates. They kept on selling features, advantages, and benefits. They were used to the steady sales of 1974-77. Even though many had been through the tough times of 1971-73, Doug was the only one who took the time to find out how others had succeeded during that period.

So Doug is a hero, right? Unfortunately, that's wrong. He did very well, winning his company's President's award several years in a row. Unfortunately, since he didn't share his ideas with his co-workers, his division always had the worst performance record. Eventually, his division was eliminated. Although his company wanted him to move to another city to join another group, Doug refused, citing family obligations.

Although he has continued to do well in another company, he could have kept his seniority if he had helped his division and his co-workers by sharing the secrets of his success.

Share your secrets with your peers? Am I crazy? (Yes, but it doesn't apply here.) "Success shared is success squared." Yeah, it's corny, but you'll never forget it. It took me a long time to realize it, but every time I shared a "secret" with a fellow employee, I thought of an even better idea and/or technique. There is nothing wrong with using it first, reaping the benefits, rising to the top, and then sharing that killer new technique with everyone. That way everybody wins. If you study and model most successful people, you will find that virtually every one of them shared their great ideas and vision. It's a big part of what made them successful.

The quote, "There's no limit to what a person can achieve as long as he or she doesn't care who takes the credit," is attributed to literally hundreds of people... hundreds of successful people, including one of my top role models, Mary Kay Ash. It's an excellent philosophy to model. There is much more about this concept later in the book.

For now, let's get back to learning from the past. Military leaders have always studied the strategy of famous battles. And until the last ten years, they didn't have the convenience and speed of the Internet. Today, researching past successes in any field is relatively easy. And you can always take a break and bid on that Lone Ranger lunchbox you've always wanted.

Prior to my 15 years at QVC, I spent several years during the 1980's as a Creative Director for a Marketing and Advertising Agency in Atlanta. It was there that I learned the value of studying past successes. I first "discovered" this concept when the City of Atlanta hired us to promote them as a convention and tourist center.

I spent several days trying to create the perfect ad campaign. My Exxon word processor (state-of-the-art for that time) was cranking out pages overtime. (I'm almost convinced that my "We Cleaned Up Real Nice Since the Big Fire" campaign would have been prime for a Clio.) Every idea seemed to be worse than the one before it. How do you market a city that's huge, growing by leaps and bounds and diverse?

"I Love New York." What a great song. I heard one of

NYC's musical spots on the radio while driving home. New York, they're huge, growing by leaps and bounds, diverse. That's it. "I Love Atlanta." Okay, so after the copyright infringement suit, maybe I could get a job selling vacuum cleaners door-to-door.

But...if I had an original song written for Atlanta, one that captured the spirit of the city as well as the New York anthem did for the Big Apple, I'd really have something. We wrote and produced a song that dripped with southern charm but didn't have too much of a country sound. It could have been one of the first country "crossover" songs, having enough musical diversity to appeal to a wide audience. The city fathers loved it, paid us a bundle for the rights and hired us to produce the promotional campaign. The song, "Atlanta, You've Got a Way About Your Style," was an extremely important part of a successful campaign.

I realized that what I had done was called "modeling," an already proven creative technique. I had always thought it was too simplistic to be truly effective. I took what had worked someplace else, the "I Love New York song, and customized it for another situation and viola: success!

While every example of modeling wasn't going to be that easy, it still worked almost every time I used it. Finding a truly similar situation to model is the most difficult part. Once you find it, the rest is relatively easy.

QVC was the most wonderful learning laboratory for sales techniques. As one of their original on-air hosts, I had the opportunity to really perfect the modeling technique. But first, you might be asking just how a nerdy-looking guy can become the best selling salesperson on the nation's largest cable shopping channel?

How had other "unlikely" candidates in the public eye gotten a chance in the past? That was a question I had to answer before I went for the audition. I was up against some of the best-looking media people in the country; I had to stand out in a very positive way.

Back in 1986, without the Internet, I scoured both the marketing and media sections of the main library in Philadelphia. There were lots of examples of how an ordinary product generated extraordinary sales. The writings of David Oglevy and other advertising gurus of the time were helpful, but none of the techniques could be adapted to my situation.

In several movie books, I read about the unbelievably creative things done by many leading actors and actresses to land the "perfect role." But most of these people were trading on their glamour and good looks and I had...a lot of sales ability and creativity. On the Bo Derek scale of beauty, I always considered myself to be a 3...on a good day.

I took a break at the library and read a section in a book about TV shows. I've always been a big TV junkie. I thought it would be a mindless diversion. But in a chapter devoted to the breakthrough drama Hill Street Blues, I found out how Bruce Weitz auditioned for the role of Detective Mick Belker. Since the character of Detective Belker was a tough-as-nails, street-smart undercover cop, Weitz went in dressed in character, grubby, needing a shave (and looking like he needed a shower). When Weitz was called, he barged into the casting director's office and jumped on his desk, knocking everything off in the process. He then proceeded to act as menacing as possible, answering almost every question with a threatening grunt.

It worked! He made an impression as someone who had done his homework about his character. His unconventional audition made him difficult to forget. He played Belker for several successful seasons, winning an Emmy as best supporting actor.

What did his unconventional audition have to do with my getting the job at QVC? Like Weitz, I faced some pretty fierce competition. How could I stand out (in a good way) among a bunch of great looking, model types? Like Weitz, I learned my "character." I was going to be a retail salesperson, selling mostly jewelry in those early days of televised shopping. I learned as much about gold, silver and gemstones as I could, immersing myself in my character much the same way Weitz had done. Then, I had the "money idea."

I've been a magic and sleight-of-hand enthusiast for a long time. Adding that to the fact that in the early days of the industry, televised shopping shows placed great stock in the fact the "supplies are limited, call in now," I came up with a plan. If they gave me a piece of jewelry for the audition, I would dazzle them with the knowledge I could share with the viewers and then make it vanish.

I went to QVC wired with every vanishing device and technique known to modern man. I sat down in front of the cameras and they handed me a pencil, telling me to sell it for five minutes. I was very familiar with this common test of basic salesmanship. I held my own, giving a litany of features and benefits for the pencil. Then, I looked right at the camera and said, "But supplies are limited and if you don't call in now, it'll be gone." It vanished perfectly, going up a virtually invisible thread that ran up my sleeve and was attached to a spring-loaded reel. They all laughed and did their own vanishing act, walking into the control room. I figured magic wasn't the sort of thing they were looking for and they were going to come back and give me the "don't call us, we'll call you," routine.

After a few minutes they came back into the studio and handed me a gold chain to sell. I did my best to dazzle them with all the facts about gold percentages in 14 karat gold, scarcity of the metal as well as some historic trivia about gold. Then, using a totally different technique than I used for the pencil, I made the chain vanish, using the "limited quantity" story again. When I finished, they adjourned once more into the control room, asking me to wait a few minutes.

They came back in and admitted that they had watched the tape frame-by-frame and couldn't figure out how I had vanished the pencil or the chain. I told them that I couldn't reveal the secret (this was before all those Network TV "Magic Secrets Revealed" specials). They thanked me and said they'd be in touch.

It was the longest week I can ever remember. They called me in for a final interview and asked me if I could do the magic shtick on a regular basis. I said yes and was known as the Magic Host for my first couple of years, before the act got old and I moved on to bigger and more effective sales techniques.

QVC executives told me that the magic convinced them I could do the job. By taking the time to find out what had worked in past TV auditions and customizing it for my own purposes, I beat out a lot of "pretty people." Once I had the job, I used this technique countless times for on-air presentations, outselling other hosts who were more concerned with how they looked rather than how well they sold.

Modeling became the most powerful sales technique

I used at QVC. I regularly conducted seminars for my fellow hosts, stressing the importance of the technique and sharing my latest examples. Again, by sharing what I had learned, I always came up with "bigger and better" techniques while preparing my teaching material. Some hosts embraced the ideas. Sadly, many did not. Those who came from the teleprompter-driven TV world thought it was too much work. They were happy to be on television, making a good living without working too hard. If they had realized how much QVC was paying the really successful hosts, they might have reconsidered their position.

Another interesting example of modeling came out of selling *Star Trek* memorabilia, a huge category on televised shopping shows for a few years. I'm a Trekkie, I admit it. Actually, I wasn't the first host chosen to sell *Star Trek* merchandise. The host who did the first *Star Trek* shows did extremely well. However, once the newness wore off, sales of *Star Trek* chachkas dropped dramatically. Try as he might, the host was missing the mark with the audience.

My on-air schedule was pretty full, which is why I hadn't been scheduled for the shows in the first place.

Faced with the loss of what had been a very profitable product line, they asked me to host a show. I had about a month. I would have a guest, Jonathan Frakes, who was playing Commander Ryker on *Star Trek: The Next Generation*.

My first stop was a science fiction convention. Even with my lifelong sci-fi fandom, I had yet to experience this phenomenon. I wanted to find out what made people buy expensive "collectible" stuff. What an experience!

First of all, you pay about a $20 admission for the "privilege" of walking among aisles and aisles of science fiction memorabilia. Wow! I was in heaven! I saw things from movies and TV shows that were several decades old...but I remembered them when they were new. Okay, I'm a rapidly aging geek. But I was having fun. Modeling is work, but many times it turns out to be enjoyable.

Okay, I had to find out what was motivating the attendees to buy. My olfactory senses told me that some of them didn't shower regularly. While it was an interesting, somewhat unpleasant revelation, it was not the kind of information I needed.

After speaking to several people at the convention, a picture began to develop. These people loved to know things that no one else knew. Behind-the-scenes knowledge was a valuable commodity. Possessing it meant you were worthy of respect. I had the feeling that it was the only way many of theses fans thought they could get respect.

Behind-the-scenes-information was the key. I spent several hours at the convention, gathering as much information as I could. Rumors abound at a gathering like that. However, Paramount Studios licensed the *Star Trek* shows. They hated unsubstantiated rumors, especially when they gave away a surprise ending or told some fact they'd rather not have in the public domain. I had to edit the information I got, actually clearing much of it with Paramount.

I also used a great deal of the information to craft my questions for Jonathan Frakes. These questions would reveal enough behind-the scenes info to titillate even the most die-hard fan. I made sure to stress this fact in all the promotion for the upcoming show.

Jonathan turned out to be very nice and extremely entertaining. He was open, honest, and very funny. The show was a hit; the sales were back. I've always maintained that since the invention of the remote control, people (especially men) watch TV with their thumbs. If it's not entertaining...ZAP! The viewer "thumbs" to another channel. Our show was entertaining and was modeling one of the main reasons that sci-fi fans go to conventions—information! I found out what worked in another venue and translated it to our medium.

We did get into a little trouble by revealing a few things Paramount would rather have kept under wraps at the time. However, our sales more than made up for a few minor transgressions. During the next few years, I hosted many more extremely successful *Star Trek* shows, "dishing as much dirt" as I could without alienating the executives at Paramount (and QVC). I was the plastic phaser king! Modeling—the final frontier.

I also used modeling to increase the sales of musical instruments on QVC. As a lifelong musician, I thought the category was a slam-dunk. I had a very nice electric guitar package (guitar, amplifier, and some accessories) on the show. While I'm no Eric Clapton, I can hold my own. I opened the sell with the flashiest licks I could muster out of my middle-aged fingers.

Everyone in the studio was impressed. Unfortunately, the viewer was not. Sales were dismal, so bad that they considered eliminating the category altogether. I blew it, assuming that my pre-existing knowledge and ability would make the product irresistible. Hey, when I'm wrong, I'm wrong.

They told me the guitar package had one more opportunity to succeed. Homework time! I headed to the one of the most successful music stores in the area to see what motivated people to buy. My first impression was a real eye opener. Almost every guitar salesperson I observed was doing exactly the same thing I had done on-air. And some of these men and women could really play. I witnessed an amazing display of speed and fingerboard pyrotechnics. I was impressed and so were the customers. However, most left the store without making a purchase.

Posing as a customer (which I often was in music stores), I asked the store manager if I could be helped by his best salesperson. He obliged, and I was soon perusing an impressive display of fine guitars with a nice looking, well-groomed (which made him stand out among his peers) young man. He asked what style I played and I told him I was partial to the blues. He took down a guitar and proceeded to play one hell of a blues lick. So far, it was the same ineffective technique the other salespeople and I had used. Then, it changed.

"Sit down and I'll show you how I did it," he said. I learned a new technique and it didn't cost me a thing. He then played another impressive riff and showed me how to play it as well. I found myself wanting the guitar, even though I already owned several others. But this one was easier to play. Actually, the salesperson had shown me a few techniques that just made it seem that way. In fact, I did return to the store a few days later and actually bought the new guitar from him. I still have it and play it all the time. Like most salespeople, after a great sales presentation, I love to buy!

But along with a new musical instrument, I gained a powerful insight about selling musical instruments. It's okay to "dazzle" your customers as long as you show them how to "dazzle" their audience.

Make it worth their while to watch. I'm a good player myself, but no one is going to buy a guitar so they can play like me...unless I can show him or her how easy it is and how much fun it is.

It took some time to figure out what I could show a beginner that would make him or her want to buy the guitar. I finally hit upon the idea of showing the audience how to play a basic rock and blues background, the structure of which would allow them to play literally thousands of popular and familiar songs. For the more advanced player, I came up with a somewhat intricate riff, actually an adaptation of the one I had been taught at the music store.

I used this technique in the next presentation, and it worked like a charm. The guitar sold out and became a successful, recurring product for quite some time. Impressed by my "educational" on-air presentation, a vendor offered me the chance to write and produce a how-to guitar video for the QVC customer. I did, and it sold over 50,000 copies, making it one of the most successful guitar instructional videos of that time. Sometimes modeling takes you to some very unexpected, interesting, and profitable places.

In 15 years at QVC, I saw the good, bad, and ugly of product vendors. I'll never forget the 6'-10" guy (I'm 5'-11") who did an entire presentation looking right at the camera, never acknowledging I was there. What did I do? Since we had worked out a very entertaining and informative presentation before we went on-air and this guy had decided he knew best, I "gave him enough rope." I saw no sense in trying to fight him. That would have involved the viewer in a very uncomfortable situation. His product failed so badly that, like the man who rode the MTA, he never returned.

However, some vendors were masters of modeling. For example, Tony Robbins lives it and preaches it. He credits his success in many aspects of his life to successfully modeling what has worked in the past. Another example is David Oreck, a heroic aviator during World War II, who had the opportunity to study the highly efficient factories in Post-War Germany. He modeled that efficiency and created the most successful American-made vacuum cleaner (and vacuum cleaner company) in the world.

Some individuals are natural born salespeople, but these are few and far between. Arthur Godfrey was one of those people. Though he had no formal training in the world of sales, he had what some media types call "it." Even people who use the word can't really define "it," but they know "it" when they see "it."

Godfrey was so credible that it's rumored that he was chosen by President Dwight Eisenhower to record a message for Conelrad, the civil defense department that was the precursor of the current Emergency Broadcast System. (Conelrad was an acronym that stood for control of electronic radiation.)

Although briefly mentioned in a story that appeared in *Time* magazine back in the 1950's, no actual transcription of this announcement has even been found. However, it is widely believed that Godfrey announced something like, "The country is under atomic attack, all measures are being taken to defend the population and, most importantly, we WILL survive." His credibility and sales ability made him a natural for this. (The fact that he was a good friend of President Eisenhower didn't hurt.)

Godfrey's natural sales talents made him the original broadcast "pitchman." Oh, to have been a fly on the wall when he made them get him a hot bowl of Lipton soup to eat on the air. You can just hear everyone from the interns to the executives screaming, "But this is radio, they'll never see it!" He made such a convincing presentation for the "steaming bowl of delicious soup, with tender noodles swimming in a hot, flavorful broth. If she still had the time, Mom would make it this good."

Lipton sales soared that day, well beyond anyone's expectations. One can only imagine the litany of products he was asked to consume on the air after that.

I was able to model this technique during a radio appearance. I love radio and have done shows since I was a teenager. During a fill-in show a few years ago, the sponsor was a local coffee roaster. I made a fresh pot of coffee right before going on-air. When it came time for the commercial, I poured the coffee into the cup, slowly and deliberately, and started my pitch. "I wish you could see the steaming, rich, dark Morningstar coffee pouring into my favorite mug, and experience the marvelous aroma of the steam that's enveloping the microphone. It smells so delicious." I then took a sip. "Have you ever wanted a coffee that tastes as good as it smells?

That's Morningstar Coffee! Smooth, rich...I don't usually drink my coffee black, but this one is so delicious, it doesn't need a thing." I finished by giving the company facts, telling everyone where they could get the coffee, and made a "call to action" (see the chapter of the same name).

Their sales skyrocketed in the listening area. I just modeled what Godfrey did, applied it to my product and situation, and the sales rolled in.

Arthur Godfrey is one of my heroes. Not his personal life, but his professional career and style. I model his techniques whenever I can. I also have a great admiration for P.T. Barnum. Phineas Taylor Barnum was another of history's great salespeople. Contrary to popular belief, he never said, "There's a sucker born every minute." David Hannum, one of Barnum's competitors, uttered that phrase and Barnum, the more famous of the two, got the unfortunate credit.

Barnum loved and respected his customers. They made him a wealthy man, and he never forgot it. If you went to Barnum's Hippodrome in Manhattan, spent the entire day and then complained that you didn't get your money's worth, your money would be refunded. You would probably have received a free pass for your next visit as well.

Sure, this was the same man who put half a doll on the tail of a fish and called it *The Fiji Mermaid* and had a group of New York musicians billed as *The Genuine Swiss Bell Choir* (They WERE playing Swiss Bells. Barnum couldn't convince the Swiss musicians to make the trip to America). People have always loved to be fooled. Back in the days before satellite TV, staring at a pickled "mermaid" in a jar was as good as it got for some people. Barnum was the consummate showman and salesman. By the way, he added more words and phrases to the English language than anyone else since. A few examples: *Jumbo*, his name for his mammoth elephant; *throwing your hat in the ring*, created when a local politician did just that to announce his candidacy at Barnum's circus; *rain or shine*, an advertising phrase created to promote Barnum's shows *under the big top*, and *Siamese Twins*, while today politically incorrect, the term used for the conjoined twins featured at Barnum's sideshow, who were said to be from Siam.

Okay, so when did I sell the Swiss Bells or offer stereopticons showing 3-D views of the *Fiji Mermaid*? Obviously that never happened, although some products came close, especially in the early days. But I did model Barnum's dedication to his customers. Without that, he would never have risen to the meteoric heights he achieved.

Have you ever taken the time to study someone, a group or something that was successful? I'm amazed how many people haven't taken the time to do this. It's very enlightening. Even if you've never done it before, think of someone or something you admire. Now ask yourself how (insert name here) became so successful. Whether it's a person, group, or product, you're already on your way to modeling success.

How does this person, group, or product apply to your life or career? Looking for a successful relationship? Been divorced? More than once? Ever studied a successful relationship? I didn't think so.

People always tell you the way they want to be "sold." The facts are riddled through history. Times change, products change, people's needs change...but basic human thinking has been the same before man took his first upright step (probably headed to the store.)

How many times have we all heard the quote from the Book of Ecclesiastes, "What has been is what will be, and what has been done is what will be done, there is nothing new under the Sun." It took me a long time to realize it applies across the board in life. Billions and billions of people have walked the face of this planet. We can learn a lot from each one of them, especially the ones who have been extremely successful.

Take the example of *American Idol*. It's a cultural phenomenon! How did they come up with such an incredible idea? I've heard so many people say, "It's such a simple idea. Why didn't I think of that?" Actually, someone thought of it a long time ago.

The *Major Bowes Amateur Hour* debuted on radio in 1935, with Ted Mack eventually taking over and moving into television. Chuck Barris took the concept into the 1970's with *The Gong Show*, a wacky show for wacky times. Things are harder and edgier in the early 21st Century. *American Idol* is harder and edgier than any previous on-air talent competition and takes full advantage of today's advanced telecommunications, network, and computer technology. Consciously or subconsciously, *American Idol* owes its genesis to modeling what has worked before in the world of broadcast amateur competitions.

Model success wherever you find it. Nothing in life is a sure thing, but this is about as close as it gets.

Call To Action...The Most Important Sales Call You'll Ever Make!

I was the perfect candidate for the job. AT&T had been a client for years. As the Creative Director for their ad agency, I knew their business as well as anyone in their organization. The interview went extremely well. Called back for two more interviews, I knew I had the job. When they hired someone else, I was truly shocked.

I sat down at the computer, where I have always done some of my best "thinking," and tried to reconstruct the entire affair. Good eye contact, great answers to their questions, new suit, not too dressy, not too casual. Given the title of this chapter, you probably realize what I did wrong; I forgot to "ask for the sale."

With my extensive background in advertising and marketing, I forgot the most important thing: Always ask for the sale! While I was very clear about what I could do for the company, putting my benefits first, I never came out and said, "I really want to work for you."

I sort of said it ("I know I could add a lot of value to your organization"), but almost only counts in horse-shoes, hand grenades, and atomic bombs.

"How soon can I start?" Sure, it might sound pushy, but I found out years later that AT&T thought I didn't really want the job. I was a very successful Creative Director for a leading agency at the time. The people interviewing me thought I was just fishing, and had no intentions of leaving my current job. However, this position, Vice President of Marketing, offered 40% more than I was making and a much better career path. If I had only asked for the job.

In my opinion, the number one reason anyone loses a sale is because he or she forgets to ask for it. In my 15 years at QVC, I saw it time and time again. And sometimes, I was the guilty party.

Computers are great sellers on televised shopping. The plethora of computer infomercials a few years back helps to prove that statement. My record of selling 11 million dollars worth of computers in one hour on QVC has not been broken in the many years since I left.

I'm very proud of that, considering that QVC is received in over 10 million more homes since I worked there.

Selling computers on television helped to show me how important it is to ask for the sale. The first computer sold on QVC, a major brand 386 (state-of-the-art for the time), sold out with just a mention. It was the early 90's and people were beginning to realize they needed a computer. And most people were buying their first.

The price was right and the demand was great. One mention and several hundred computers sold. When we got it back in stock, everyone was cocky, myself included. I prepared a very glitzy demo along with several benefits-first selling points. The demo ran flawlessly, which was great considering how easily those old machines would lock up and/or crash.

The result? We sold 75% fewer computers than we had when it sold out. And this time, it cost us 20 minutes of airtime on a medium that has to do several thousand dollars per minute just to "keep the lights on." As someone who had owned a computer since the early 80's (a VIC-20), I was shocked that my perfect demo had failed.

Just like the previous example, I was so involved with the presentation itself, I forgot to ask for the sale. Unfortunately, many times people in direct response television are guilty of not asking for the sale. Paradigms reign supreme, especially at many of the major shopping networks. While the fact that an item sold out before is a powerful motivator (scarcity), it is not the end all-be-all that some believe it to be. It doesn't take the average viewer long to figure out that if an item sells out, most times it will return in a few weeks.

I watched the video of my computer presentation. You can imagine my embarrassment when I realized that my major mistake was failing to ask for the sale. "You've seen what it can do for you and your family, why not buy this computer now? With a 30-day unconditional return policy, you have nothing to lose. It will make your life easier and more fun."

While the "return policy" angle can be overdone (so much so that it encourages renting an expensive product), used sparingly, it is a powerful motivator. It's like all sales tools; it loses its impact if you overdo it.

The next computer presentation was going to be done

by someone who wasn't very comfortable with high-tech products. I have always believed that a skill shared is a skill squared. Almost every time I teach a technique, I come up with one that's even more effective. I taught the host everything I could about presenting the computer and made sure that throughout the presentation he would ask for the sale.

Setting a record for dollar-per-minute sales in the company, the presentation was a smashing success. In an industry built upon the sales of jewelry and impulse chachkas, selling several hundred thousand dollars of an expensive high-tech item helped to prove the broad appeal and viability of televised shopping.

Along with an in-depth demonstration, the host asked for the sale, like the old axiom says about voting, "early and often." Every few minutes, he looked right at the camera and asked the customers to purchase the computer for themselves and their families.

"Early and often?" That's right. As soon as the customer knows what you're selling, you should ask for the sale. Obviously, overdone it can be extremely obnoxious.

However, experience has taught me that if you go more than a few minutes in any sales presentation without asking for the sale, you're asking for failure.

Ron Popeil, whom I'm proud to call a friend, is great at this. While his infomercials have the usual call to action (CTA) segments every few minutes, he also does it during his demos. "Buy these knives, if they're not the best knives you've ever owned, send them back for a complete refund. Buy these knives; you'll be glad you did."

Redundant? Yes, in fact, Ron would be the first to say it. But given his success over the decades, we should all be so redundant. I was once involved with an infomercial producer who literally lived and died by paradigms. He wouldn't allow me to make a call to action in the body of the infomercial, since he was preparing the standard CTA spot that would run every 6 to 8 minutes. The spot failed. Interestingly enough, by the way, only one out of every 20 infomercials ever makes money. If I were a producer, I'd have the CTA tattooed to the hosts' foreheads.

The CTA applies to all types of sales: inside, outside,

direct, broadcast...asking for the sale will increase your chances of making a sale. If you get the sale without asking for it, buy a lottery ticket because it's your lucky day.

Even though I sometimes still forget it, I learned the benefits of asking for the sale early in my career. When our advertising agency opened in Atlanta, moving there from Philadelphia in the late 70's, we had a lot to prove as the new kids in town...especially the new Yankee kids. Businesses in Atlanta had been doing just fine working with their homegrown ad agencies. And, having studied the market for quite a while before we made our move, I had great respect for the print and broadcast ads that were being produced there.

One of our first prospective clients was a software manufacturer who made an online programming and development tool. Computer networking was in its infancy, and their software made it easier, safer, and more productive for companies to link their computers.

The company wanted to produce a film demo of the system. Many long-term Atlanta agencies were also bidding on the project that involved the writing and production of a 45-minute film.

During our meeting to discuss our proposal, I asked for the sale. "You like our treatment, you know we have experience in this area, let us make this film for you. We'll do what it takes to make it the best film we've ever produced."

That's pretty close to an exact quote. I remember it because it was the Friday before Labor Day and the company called my bluff. They said if I could have a finished script to them by Tuesday, and they liked it, we'd get the job. Bye-bye Labor Day plans, hello Atlanta Public Library where I spent several hours the next day getting versed in the basics of current computer software terminology.

I'm not mentioning this to show you that I'm dedicated and a fast learner. Rather, I want you to realize that asking for the sale comes with responsibilities, sometimes very involved and unpleasant responsibilities. When I asked for the sale, I didn't qualify it by saying, "Let us produce this film for you. We can start the day after Labor Day." Yeah, that would have shown real dedication.

I finished the script as the sun was rising on Tuesday. I showered, changed into my corporate garb, and headed off to the agency. The client loved the script and we got the job. I asked for the sale and we got it and did what it took to get the job done.

Possibly inspired by my sacrifice (which now seems very small in retrospect), our production team worked almost around-the-clock and made a great film. We went on to win several awards for writing and producing a funny and entertaining film about a very dry subject.

It could have been a deadly dull film. Even the most dedicated computer programmer would be hard pressed to stay awake during a 45-minute software demo film. I came up with the idea of using vocal impressionists, to have the voice of Jack Benny talking about saving money, George Burns discussing saving time, and General Patton speaking about security. By the way, it worked so well the software company was purchased by an industry giant, making millionaires out of the young programmers. I love a win/win scenario.

Asking for the sale is probably the most important sales technique there is, but it can be overdone. Some automobile salespeople ask too often and too vehemently. If I hear "What can I do to get you in this car today?" one more time, I'm going back to my mountain bike.

I detailed several car-buying incidents in my book *Sales Magic*. I've purchased two cars since then, and things haven't changed much. While I have great respect for the men and women who earn their living as professional salespeople, I despise people who use harassment and badgering as their primary sales tools.

In *Sales Magic*, along with the awful experiences I detailed about shopping for a new car, I also told a story about a great car salesperson. His name is Steve and he is one of the most gifted and professional sales professionals I have even met. He's well-respected by his customers and peers alike and has worked for the same company for over a decade. Unfortunately, the cars he sells no longer meet my personal and professional needs, so I have to purchase my cars from another dealership. I have yet to find his equal and have added many more horror stories to my lexicon.

A car is the second largest purchase most of us will ever make. Why does the experience have to be so miserable? There are some great car salespeople who earn a fine living by providing excellent customer service and giving their customers the best possible prices. Unfortunately, that's the exception rather than the rule.

During my last new car search, I found a few who reminded me of the warden in *The Shawshank Redemption*. Sure, they asked for the sale, making me feel like a fool each time they did. "How much do you want to pay per month?" As abhorrent as I find this question to be, regardless of the circumstances, it doesn't apply to me as I have always saved up until I can pay cash for a vehicle. I also find the classic "What can I do to earn your business?" to be equally objectionable, addressing the needs of the dealership with no regard to what the customer needs.

"But that's the way we've always done it." God save us all from paradigms, but that's usually the response you'll get if you question a bad salesperson's techniques (or lack thereof).

These days when I'm shopping for a car, I arrive at the dealership with a one-page list I call "Ways to Lose My Business." It covers everything from "I will not speak with your manager or wait while you do," "I will not speak with your extended warranty manager," (if it's such a good car, why does it need an extended warranty?) and all the other hassles we've come to know and hate. It also states, "I will not haggle"; their first quoted price should be the deciding factor.

During a recent car shopping experience, I was asked to leave the first two dealerships I visited as soon as I handed them the list. Number three was the charm. The salesperson read my list and said, "I hate these things, too. I promise you, it won't happen here." Whether or not he was placating me, at least he didn't ask me to leave.

Then, he asked for the sale. "I'm sure you've checked the Internet and know the dealer cost for this car. You'll find our prices reflect a fair profit. What car would you like to try on for size?" His approach was subtle, but within two minutes, I was test-driving the car I wanted.

When I got back (he allowed me a solo drive), he asked me how I liked it, and then said, "I checked while you were gone, I can offer you that car for $XX,XXX; what do you think?" Again, he asked for the sale, more directly this time. The price represented a substantial reduction from the sticker price (which it should). He then said, "Would you like to use our financing or do you have your own?" My list didn't mention how I would be paying for the car. He assumed nothing. I was beginning to like this guy.

"I'm paying cash. If I write you the check right now, how soon can I drive out?" I asked.

"Should take a half an hour, maybe even faster," he replied. It took about 25 minutes before I was driving off the dealer's lot. He wasn't as customer-oriented as Steve had been, but he was the best I've encountered since. If I'm looking for the same type of car in a few years, I'll seek him out. He asked for the sale without badgering, harassing, or belittling me. Without asking me how he could do it, he earned my business by asking for the sale.

Getting back to QVC, while I wasn't particularly known as a jewelry salesperson, I did set a few jewelry records. Regardless of the product, I've always maintained that selling is selling. If you know how to sell, you can sell anything. Sure, passion sells better than almost anything, but even if you don't have passion for a particular product or service, you can share your customer's passion.

QVC had a truly unique piece of jewelry on the air one day. While it was stunning, compared to most jewelry that QVC offered, it was really outside-the-box. It was a necklace that featured a striking combination of freshwater pearls, gold, and gemstones. It had sold poorly all day. Even QVC's top jewelry salespeople couldn't move the item.

So what could a high tech geek like me do? I watched the tapes of presentations from two of our heavy hitters. Neither had asked for the sale. Both did an excellent job of "painting the picture," creating desire and establishing value.

I went on the air with the product and did my best to set the mood and let people know how special the piece was. Then I asked for the sale, "Order this now. Think of how you'll feel when you open the box." I also said, "Order this now. In a few days, imagine the impression you'll make when you walk into a room."

I asked for the sale several times during the presentation, and at 4'o'clock in the afternoon (not a particularly hot time in televised shopping) I wound up with the top sale of the day to that point. When I got off the air, I told the producers to tell the hosts following me to ask for the sale. I explained the concept and wrote out a few notes for the upcoming hosts. They used it and sales got better and better as the day progressed.

While I still prefer selling high tech items and cookware, it's nice to know I can hit a "change-up" when it comes across the plate. "But if I ask for the sale, the customers will think I'm pressuring them." Sure they will, if you do it too often. A lot of salespeople want to be liked (don't we all?) and view any sales technique as high pressure. Any technique can be high pressure. Even the "I want to be your friend" technique can come off as high pressure if you are too insistent about it.

I once worked on a radio sales show with someone (a highly degreed professional) who tried to come off as everyone's friend. He refused to let me use any sales techniques when I worked with him. "People don't want to be sold, they want to be your friend," he would tell me. It's a good thing I have a strong stomach. This guy came off slicker than wet Teflon.

For a while, his customers bought it. His products sold out almost every time he was on the air. He didn't ask for the sale and neither did I. His products supposedly made you feel better, act younger, lose weight, let you levitate and read minds. Okay, so maybe I exaggerated about those last two. While his products were fine, certainly did some good and didn't harm anyone, he made it seem like they were the Fountain of Youth and Alchemist's Stone all wrapped up in one.

To quote the song *Puff, the Magic Dragon*, "Then one day, it happened..." The Food and Drug Administration (FDA) and the Federal Trade Commission (FTC) issued strict guidelines about certain product claims, the same ones this man had been making for years.

While there was nothing dangerous about the claims "Everyone's Friend" was making, now according to government regulations, they were gross exaggerations. With the new rules, he could no longer promise the sun, moon, and stars. The regulations were so strict, rightfully so, he thought he couldn't even promise clouds on a rainy day! His next few sales presentations failed miserably.

After a few failures, he went into sales overdrive. Now, he wasn't everyone's friend; he was everyone's salesman. "Buy this now, before it sells out!" "Buy this now because I don't know when I'll be back." That last one was pretty accurate. His sales were so dismal that he wasn't back...ever.

There's never anything wrong with asking for the sale. But when you've spent years hyping the fact that you're everyone's friend, it's almost impossible to be taken seriously as the guy on the street corner opening his suitcase to peddle his wares. Maybe if he had worked on softening his claims so they met the new guidelines and let me do the selling, things would have been different.

Unfortunately, he panicked about his poor sales and oversold everything. People who had known him as a friend now saw him as a carny pitchman. It was an impossible and unprofitable transition.

Asking for the sale is so basic that many of us forget to do it when we get wrapped up in the sales process. Even though I've done it for decades, you've seen from the previous examples there were times when I simply forgot. Now I make it part of my checklist before any sales situation.

Whether I'm selling on television, radio, in person, or simply selling myself in a social situation, I make a quick list of the basics (mentally, most times). For me, these basics are benefits and asking for the sale. When I remember those, everything else falls into place. What would be on your list?

But That's the Way We've Always Done It
(And Other Tales of Premature Aging)

People not only fear change, they will do almost anything to prevent it. Since the definition of insanity is doing the same thing over and over again and expecting a different result, change is one of the most necessary factors to increase sales regardless of what you're selling. To that end, I'd like to start off with a tale I call, "Barbie Jell-O Wrestling." This is one of my favorite stories.

During my first 4 years as a QVC show host, I was relegated to the overnight shift. In both my appearance and presentation style, I was way too unorthodox for the current management. They had me working five, four-hour shifts each week, from midnight to 4 a.m.

In those early days, we didn't have that many products and repetition was a way of life, so much so that every night for several months in the 3 a.m. hour, I had to present a "Barbie Dream Pool Set."

It consisted of Barbie, her friend Midge, Ken the lifeguard (complete with lifeguard stand and whistle) and an 18-inch diameter, four-inch deep above-ground pool. Above-ground pool? As successful as Barbie was, I always thought she could have afforded one of those built-in jobs. I quickly realized that questioning. Barbie's design taste would probably not have increased sales, so I never mentioned it on-air.

I was bored out of my mind having to sell the same product at the same time night after night. So were my customers. Sales on the toy were steadily dropping. When I asked for some new products, I was told, "We don't put new products in the overnight shifts."

I had to do something. I have never been one to sit back and let things fail if I had the slightest opportunity to change them. I had a plan. Did I present it to those same forward-thinking bastions of corporate genius who had completely dismissed the overnight time slot? What do you think? The old adage, "It's better to beg forgiveness than ask permission" was all the authority I needed. Keep in mind, to paraphrase Sir Isaac Newton, any unauthorized actions will always have some very authorized and more than equal reactions.

I knew I could be fired. But, after some serious planning, I felt the results could be worth the risks.

On my way to the studio one night, I stopped at a local grocery store and bought a few pounds of lime Jell-O cubes (The lime green color was a perfect contrast to the dolls' colorful bathing suits). I kept the cubes in a plastic bag and right before the airing, I dumped them into the pool. As the cameras came up for the standard 3 a.m. airing of the product, I proceeded to narrate the Jell-O pool grudge match between Barbie and Midge. Ken was the referee. My narration rivaled the most vociferous and outrageous professional wrestling announcer.

It was a heated match. I acted it out with all the enthusiasm of a youngster playing with a new toy. Boy, did Midge fight dirty. And Ken never saw her illegal moves, indicating the possibility of an interesting action-figure love triangle. The bout went on for a few minutes with the cameras following every move more precisely than I had witnessed on the most demanding professional sporting events. Obviously, the crew had been as bored as I.

I stopped the match, with Ken finally calling a third foul on Midge and declaring Barbie the winner by default. Love does conquer all. I immediately went to a very strong call to action, saying, "If a 38 year-old man can have this much fun on national TV, think of the fun your children are going to have with this set."

Instead of grossing the usual $15-20,000, the $39.99 product did many times that, selling out completely. This amount was unheard of at that time, especially in the overnight hours. I was both a hero and in deep trouble at the same time.

The next day, I was called into the office and asked, "What kind of people were you selling to?"

"The kind of people who have $39.99 to spend," I answered. They were not amused, although I found out later they were impressed that I took full responsibility for the incident and defended my actions with a sound argument. Bottom line? I was soundly chewed out and told that if I ever did anything like that again I would be fired on the spot. Since I wasn't one for repeating a stunt that was okay. I had other unusual ideas to explore.

Luckily, a new management team was hired a few months later. These were the kind of people who appreciated creativity, especially when it resulted in much better sales. I knew that if the old guard had stayed in power at QVC, my days were numbered. But I didn't let it stifle my creativity. The new management team liked my different but professional approach to sales and started scheduling me in prime time slots where I began to set new sales records.

If I had given in to my natural survival urges and done the same old, same old presentations that everyone else was doing, I might still be working overnights on a televised shopping channel. Every reward has some element of risk. Usually, the greater the reward, the greater the risk.

I'm not telling you to go off half-cocked and try some wacky sales technique without careful consideration. But if you carefully plan your new techniques and are willing to accept the inherent risks, you will go far.

Consider the story of Joe Girard. He is one of my mentors and sales heroes.

If you haven't already, read everything you can from this man. He is a sales genius and real paradigm buster at the same time. He has sold more new cars than any one person in history, averaging at least one per day for decades. That's in an industry where selling a few cars a month makes you a superstar.

One of my favorite Joe Girard stories is from his early days. He was sitting around the dealership listening to the other salespeople complain about how slow sales had been. He chose not to add his voice to the tales of woe, opting to do things very differently.

Armed with a pocket full of business cards, he went door-to-door, introducing himself and giving out his business card. The customers didn't come into the dealership, so he went to them. It was brilliant and just one of the many ways Joe Girard went on to become the greatest car salesperson in the world. Again, read everything you can find from this man.

Paradigms are tough to break, especially if it's a paradigm from a very successful company. Let me offer another example. In the 1940's and 50's, a time when the railroads were some of the most profitable businesses in this country, they foolishly gave up the opportunity to own most of the trucking companies and airlines because they were "Railroad Men." They didn't see themselves in their real business, which was transportation.

Think of how different the world would be today if the railroad companies had invested in trucking and air transportation. By steadfastly adhering to their elitism as "railroad men," they sealed their fate. Without massive government subsidies, most passenger railroads would not be in business today.

IBM is another sad tale of "that's the way we've always done it." It's amazing to realize that a company with the one-word corporate credo of "Think," would give up the rights to the DOS operating system for their computers. But they did. Actually, in a historic meeting with a young and nearly broke Bill Gates, they literally turned up their noses at all software. They believed that there was no money in software. The real profit in computers would be in hardware. They left software to the code writers of the day, most of whom they assumed to be "hippie freaks" with little drive or desire for success.

With IBM's help, Microsoft became one of the most successful companies in the world, and Bill Gates...well, he's doing just fine. As many times as I've heard "But that's the way we've always done it," I'm still always surprised by this small-minded attitude. I saw it many times when I worked in advertising.

Our advertising agency did a great deal of work for AT&T and many of its operating companies (Baby Bells) in the late 70's and early 80's. Then, thanks to a federal Judge named Green, they were forced to divest themselves of their enormously profitable operating companies. Why?

Simply put, they had a sweet deal going and thought their corporate might could fend off any challenge. For decades, most of us had been leasing our crappy bakelite dial phones from Ma Bell, eventually paying dozens of times their retail values to the communications giant, and still we didn't own them.

AT&T also had itself declared a monopoly, so it could better serve the "public interest." It must be great to operate for decades without any competition.

To put it colloquially, they had more money than God. They weren't interested in changing with the times. They were, after all, **The Phone Company**, rich, powerful and an absolute necessity.

Some major lawsuits sought to end their monopolistic stranglehold on the nation's telecommunications. Eventually, in 1984 they were forced to divest, and their monopoly was ended. Competition was fast in coming, and soon most of us opted to own our own phones and many chose another phone company to handle our calls.

There's no way to determine what the outcome would have been if AT&T had been willing to evolve with the times. But history indicates that most companies who carefully plan to change along with their customers achieve long-term success. Imagine the public support AT&T would have received if they let us own our phones and allowed fair competition. Public support can sway legislative opinion. Obviously, AT&T is still in business but a pale reflection of what it once was.

As salespeople, in order to sell more, we need to carefully identify the opportunities to do things better.

Change is never easy; it must be meticulously planned and the consequences weighed before proceeding. As an example of this, I present the tale of "The $11,000,000 Hour."

As I have previously stated, computers have always been big business for televised shopping channels. Most have been really good values, either an overstock or closeout opportunity or savings realized from the network's purchase of a great quantity of one machine. With the exception of a few unscrupulous channels that have knowingly sold inferior computers with no regard for the impact to their customers or bottom line, computer sales on television are a win-win scenario. They usually represent great values for customers and yield excellent sales for the networks.

QVC had a quality control department who would have failed their own mother if she didn't meet specifications. Our computers were first class units that usually represented the latest technology. Near the end of my 15-year tenure there, computer sales had flattened out and were actually starting to decline. As someone who has used computers since I got my first VIC- 20 back in the early 80's, I was a real enthusiast...as long as enthusiast can be loosely interpreted as "one who really sucks at video games."

Our computer presentations had become extremely predictable. First do this and then do that. We were not just a retailer, we also a *televised retailer*. This was TV, and the delicate balance of information versus entertainment would often mean the difference between failure and success. I watched many tapes of my own computer presentations as well as those of other hosts. They were fine...boring, but fine.

I determined one thing that was standing in the way of better computer presentations was QVC's "backyard fence" philosophy. This meant all the hosts were trying to simulate the experience of your neighbor leaning over the fence and just shooting the breeze with you in a very nonchalant manner. Of course, I've never leaned over my backyard fence and said something to my neighbor like, "Hey Charlie, how about those new cubic zirconias?" Or, "The new air cleaners sure are something, aren't they?"

While I have always hated TV salespeople who sound like stereotypical carnival barkers, I still believe you have to ask for the sale if you really want it. You don't have to grab the customers by the lapel to get their attention, but you do have to close the sale. There's an entire chapter about closing the sale in this book. It's the basis for the entire sales process.

Okay, I knew I had to come up with creative ways to ask for the sale without leaving the comfort of the corporate backyard fence. What I came up with were phrases like, "Imagine how great you're going to feel when you realize how much you'll be able to do with your new computer." For real value opportunities, I would use, "Get this computer now, before the price goes up so you can enjoy everything it can do." I even came up with the line, "With a 30-day money back guarantee, you have nothing to lose and everything to gain. We're just a toll-free call away for you."

As tame as these lines sound, they were too strong for QVC's backyard fence strategy at that time. I believed if I could create a series of powerful and compelling demonstrations that had never before been done, I had earned the right to ask for the sale.

The results should be so huge that my small attempt at paradigm busting would go mostly unnoticed.

The demos were the hard part. Prior to a big computer presentation in early December, I spent weeks, at least two hours every day, creating and practicing all types of new demonstrations. One, which involved running several computer animations from the web simultaneously, is still used today later by all the televised shopping channels. I'm very proud of that. I'd be more proud if they said, "Here's the Steve Bryant demo." But, to paraphrase the late sales powerhouse Mary Kay Ash, "There's no limit to what a person can do as long as he or she doesn't care who gets the credit."

Along with the multi screen demo, I emailed the then President of Google and asked him if we could show his search engine on the air if we gave him credit. He e-mailed back his approval a few minutes later. This was actually another slam at "but that's the way we've always done it." Our legal department was supposed to do such things. But once I had Google's approval, they didn't complain...too much.

The Google demo was going to be great. Since we took

a lot of phone calls from our customers, I was going to ask them about their hobbies. When they said something like "doll collecting" I was going to do a Google search and show them the hundreds of thousands of sites devoted to doll collecting.

Along with many more demos, the big night arrived. For a full hour, I went through each new demo, asking for the sale when I thought I had shown the customer enough to earn the right, which was quite often. At the end of the hour, there was quite a wait on the phone lines for a nearly $2000 purchase. When the dust cleared, we had grossed $11,000,000 in one hour, much more than any hour in our more than 12-year history.

Unfortunately, I didn't get a lot of high fives and attaboys for my work. The network executives had heard me asking for the sale and were disappointed by my breach of conduct. They did call me in for one of those "Ward/Beaver Chats" to explain how disappointed they were with me. They asked me to tone it down and I agreed. However, I did get a nice bonus a few months later, and I'm sure it wasn't for coloring within the lines.

At the same time, with computer sales lagging again (we weren't asking for the sale), they asked me to do some sales training and allowed me to teach the hosts how to ask for the sale in a subtle, backyard fence manner. I did and once the hosts started to do new demos and ask for the sale, albeit in a subtle manner, computer sales were back on track.

Often, your rewards for thinking and acting outside-the-box don't come right away. But, if you carefully plan and execute your attack, they should come. There might be a little grief (maybe a lot) and the rewards might not be what you expected, but extraordinary sales efforts that yield extraordinary sales results should be rewarded. If they're not, it might be time to start selling yourself to another employer.

Sometimes you don't have the luxury of time to plan and execute a different sales presentation. That's where your instincts come into play. If you've studied your craft as diligently as successful salesperson should, your instincts should be excellent. Trust them; sometimes they're all you have.

One example of this is when CBS decided to move their

popular radio comedy *My Favorite Husband* to television. The radio series starred Lucille Ball and Richard Denning as her husband. When the TV offer was made, Lucy and husband Desi proposed that Desi be featured as her husband. Given the social climate in the early 50's, CBS executives balked at the thought of a Cuban as Lucy's husband, even though he was in real life.

Desi Arnez is another of my sales heroes. His success was nothing short of phenomenal. A man who started his life in this country by cleaning the bottom of birdcages wound up as a show business entrepreneur, changing the face of television forever. His sales skills were extraordinary and his work ethic impeccable. So, just what did he do when faced with CBS's unquestionably bigoted decision to exclude him from Lucy's new television show?

Since he really was Lucy's husband, I'm sure he had no idea that they would balk at his joining the cast. He was a skilled actor and musician with good credentials. The unexpected "no" from CBS brought his instincts into play. He asked if they would change their minds if he could prove to them that America would accept the pair as husband and wife. At the time, he didn't know how he was going to do it; he just knew he had the skills and determination to make it happen. They agreed, realizing the Herculean nature of his proposal should have doomed it from the start. Desi's sales skills and determination had convinced them to at least let him try.

He wrote a script and then he and Lucy toured the country performing it again and again. They received rave reviews. America fell in love with Lucy and Desi. Months later, armed with reams of excellent reviews and publicity, he approached CBS. While he hadn't yet changed the social climate of a country yet to go through the civil rights revolution, he did convince CBS that he and Lucy were a hit. They agreed and TV was never the same.

Desi also used his extensive sales skills to convince CBS to use three cameras to film the series, the same way movies were produced. It had never been done before; TV was a one-camera shoot because "that's the way we've always done it." He convinced them and TV never looked the same again.

But if he hadn't had great instincts in the first place, allowing him to make his initial offer, only her family and friends would have had the opportunity to *Love Lucy*.

Think originally, plan until it hurts, and practice so much that your new presentation is as much a part of you as your nose. Make it your business to join the fight against the saddest phrase in American business, "But that's the way we've always done it."

Customer Service, the First and Final Frontier

Everybody in sales, talks about customers. Salespeople want to know how to get more customers, ways to create customer loyalty, and methods to get existing customers to spend more. But how many salespeople know what a customer is? While the obvious answer is "A customer is someone who spends money on your products and/or services," the true definition is much more involved. Understanding this detailed definition can really help you create more and better customers.

Back before the Industrial Revolution (before 1830), most goods were made one at a time and only when requested. For example, if someone wanted a bowl, he or she would go to a potter, find a style they liked and have the bowl "custom" made. People in England who bought things in this manner became colloquially known as "customers."

While this manner of commerce seems antiquated and inefficient by today's standards, it provides a valuable template for creating tomorrow's customers. How many of us have forgotten that we need to serve the specific needs of our customers? How many of us, because of economic, space or other logistical limitations, provide only partial solutions or choices for our customers?

In today's crowded marketplace, merchants who embrace this spirit of "customization" will stand out and thereby prosper. And while online retailers are offering custom tailored clothing, the concept of customization does not have to be this involved. Once you know who your customers are, it's fairly easy to "tailor" your assortment to them.

I recently taught a class in sales to the Vanderbilt University MBA program. Students in this program are among the best and brightest in the country. When I asked them for a definition of a *customer*, their answer was the exact quote from the first paragraph of this chapter: "A customer is someone who spends money on your products and/or services." I told them that if they truly believed this, they would never have that many.

Why? Their definition described a buyer. If someone buys your products, he or she is a buyer, nothing more. If they continue to come back for more, and regularly recommend you to others, they are a *customer*. Your company is obviously meeting their custom needs. I told the Vanderbilt students that a better definition is "A customer is someone who trusts, respects, and likes your company and products enough to make regular purchases and repeatedly recommend you to associates, friends, and relatives."

QVC, now almost a $7 billion dollar company, had one basic philosophy about customer satisfaction: "Under promise and over deliver!" That was it. We established trust with our customers and did everything possible to maintain that relationship. That is one of the many reasons that QVC is nearly 3 times as profitable as HSN, even though HSN was the first national shopping network, predating QVC by several years.

Until a few years ago, listening to an HSN sales presentation would lead you to believe that everything they sold was "the best," "most beautiful," "lowest priced," "most incredible," "more stunning," "the greatest," etc. When you received the product, and it wasn't "the best...," you were disappointed and not likely to make another purchase.

On QVC, we were trained to accurately describe a product and give compelling lifestyle reasons for purchasing it. We had many things that were "beautiful," just not "the most beautiful." We had lots of "good values," but no "lowest priced in the world" products. Customers were delighted when they opened a box and found out that the product inside exceeded their expectations. They became customers in the *truest* sense. And it didn't stop there.

QVC had (and still has) a phenomenal commitment to customer service, before, during, and after the sale. Before being permitted to speak to a customer, their customer service representatives were extensively trained for weeks. This was the case whether they were taking orders or solving problems. QVC paid these people extremely well, by industry standards, and trained them constantly. Outstanding service was rewarded as quickly as bad service was disciplined.

When I started to do sales training for the hosts at QVC, I came up with an interesting way of looking at the customer service issue. "As salespeople, we are the first customer service representative our customers will encounter. If we do our jobs right, we'll most likely be the last one."

Think about it. Except for the occasional defective product, an occasional wrong size or even a bit of buyers' remorse, if you don't oversell a product and simply tell the truth without forgetting to ask for the sale, the next time your company should hear from a customer is when they want to make another purchase. When this is the case, you have provided total customer service.

But you ask, "What about competition? It's dog-eat-dog out there. I have to hype it to sell it. If I don't, someone else will, and they'll get the sale." That's truly flawed reasoning. If you really feel this way, you should be selling cars, not like the legendary gentleman Joe Girard or his peers, but like old school practitioners. Unfortunately, there are far too many of these salespeople around today in many different fields.

In my last book, *Sales Magic*, ©1993 Amherst Media (okay, I'm a procrastinator), I related several horror stories about buying a car. As I've said before, it's the second largest purchase most of us will make, and in most cases it's usually one of the worst experiences you'll ever have.

There are far too many old school hawkers still selling cars and many other types of products and services. You know the type. "How much do you want the payments to be?" (Regardless of whether you can afford them or not.) "You have to get the extended warranty." (If the car's so good, why is this necessary? Oh, that's right, to line the salesperson's and dealer's pocket.) "Let me get my manager." (Should I have been dealing with him or her right from the start?) The list is almost endless.

Have you ever asked yourself if you would buy from you? I wonder how many car salespeople ask themselves this question. I'm sure the truly great ones do. I ask it every time I do a live, on-air sales presentation or infomercial. "Would I watch and buy from me?" It's a very effective and powerful question and has helped me to maintain my sales success through the years.

If you get the opportunity, you should attend one of the "car salesmanship" classes conducted by dealers.

It's pretty obvious they think very little of their customers, or should I should say *buyers*. Most of the sales techniques they teach border on downright intimidation. In many cases, prospective car sellers are taught to belittle their customers when talking about whether or not the customer can afford the car. "Surely you can afford $500 a month, Ms. Smith?" (Of course, that's $500 a month for the rest of her adult life.)

What if these dealers taught real sales techniques and preached the gospel of cultivating customers instead of relying on "But that's the way we've always done it?" Would American and a number of foreign automakers be in the kind of trouble most are today? I don't think so.

Do you treat your customers properly? Do they feel special? Do they feel satisfied after every sale? If you didn't answer three "yeses" in a row, you're just cultivating buyers, not customers.

My dislike for old school car salespeople is well known. But a bad salesperson is a bad salesperson in any endeavor. How many do you encounter in a week, a month, last year, this year? If I asked one of your customers this question, would your name be on the list?

A true sale is a never-ending process. Remember, "You are the first customer service representative your customer will encounter." As my sales continued to grow at QVC, I took seminars and read as many books on sales and customer service as I could. Once, when my personal growth had plateaued, I broke my paradigm and started concentrating solely on customer service books, pleased to see how many of them had been written. For many years, I have asked myself, "What else can I do for my customer?" I was already creating very powerful, compelling, and entertaining presentations on QVC. Sure, I always tried to make them better, but my numbers weren't growing.

During a brainstorming session, I wrote down, "Communicate." I communicated with them on TV for a few hours each day, but did nothing else. All the hosts had dedicated people to answer the hundreds of emails we received each week. And while many of us had taken the time to write "personal" boilerplate replies, few of us took any time to personally respond. Since I sold a lot of high tech products, many of which generated a lot of calls to customer service, I saw an opportunity.

I got together with the person who answered my mail and had her forward the technical questions to me. I didn't know how many there were. Once people got their computer, digital camera, or other high tech item home, they wanted to do more than I had shown them in my on-air demo. Most were asking customer service if they could help them do more with their new technical purchase.

First of all, it was a great wake up call for my on-air demos. I started to find ways to show more "cool things" in the brief time allotted to an on-air presentation. More importantly, I started to personally answer these technical questions. For the first few weeks, it added 8-10 hours to my schedule. Soon, with my assistant's help, I was able to complete this task in about eight hours each week.

In a few weeks, I noticed my sales began to grow substantially. I did some research and found out that I was attracting more repeat customers than ever before. In fact, my repeat customer percentage was higher than anyone had ever achieved.

The extra time and effort I was putting in was working.

I kept up my personal response to e-mails for the rest of my tenure at QVC. So what did I get out of it? Along with a sense of achievement, being able to continually top my personal best, I also received extra bonuses. QVC was so grateful that they even had a custom guitar designed for me. If you are working for a good employer, your extra efforts will be rewarded. While I didn't do it for more money, it really made me feel like a valued employee.

Do you do anything extra for your customers? Something beyond the obligatory lunch, dinner, tickets to a show or sporting event? If you don't, how are your sales? Static? Worse yet, declining? Think of a way you can better communicate with your customers. Is there something they need regarding your product or service, something that's not included with their purchase? Think about it. Brainstorm; write down every idea you have. You'll probably hit on something great.

What's the cost of not doing everything possible for your customers? Of course, you could lose their business.

But more importantly, you could lose their respect. The impact of that could last forever.

To give you an example of what I mean, let me recount an incident that dates back to the 1970's. I bought my first really good stereo system when I was 20. I was in college and had worked hard to save about $1000, a lot of money for a stereo system back in 1971. But it was a dream system, complete with one of the first Dolby© cassette decks on the market. As a big music fan, and music major in college, I was really excited as I put the system together at a major stereo store near my hometown.

The salesperson helped, offering his expertise in the selection of speakers, the right cable…it was really a state-of-the-art system. Once I wrote the check for $1000, I asked the salesman to help me put the boxes in my car. He replied that he couldn't, since there was no one else on duty at the time. I pointed out the fact that my car was right in front of the store and that he would only be out for a few seconds each time. He again refused, saying that if I waited a few hours, someone else would be there and he would be able to help.

A few hours? I had to get to work, so I took the time and loaded my car. When I finished, in my youthful exuberance, I sought him out to shake his hand. He was busy on the phone. I overheard him tell his girlfriend that he had just sold "the crappiest system we have" to some hick sucker. I walked into the room and confronted him. He said he was on the phone and would be with me when he finished. While it's been 35 years since the incident, I still remember it like it was yesterday. I brought the system back into the store, again by myself, and got my money back. It was the first time I found out I could scream that loud. Today, my diatribe would be classified as "terroristic threats."

But wait, there's more...the stereo store is now a major national chain. While I'm sure they've been bought and sold a dozen times or more, I still hold a grudge against that loser who worked for them 35 years ago. I bad mouth them to people who ask for recommendations, and no matter how long I live, I will never spend a dime with them. I figure their one bad salesperson has cost them six or seven figures over the years in lost sales from my dissatisfaction and bad recommendations alone.

How many more people have they offended over the years? How many millions of dollars have they lost? I'm not a vengeful person, but the thought of it makes me smile!

How does your company handle customer complaints? No matter how good you are, you're going to get them. There's the wonderful, possibly apocryphal story concerning a Nordstrom store in Fairbanks, Alaska taking back a set of snow tires. According to the story, a store clerk cheerfully gave the customer a refund, even though they had never sold snow tires. Now whether or not this Nordstrom store was located on the site of a former tire store, as some explanations proffer, the story is rarely questioned. Nordstrom has such an excellent reputation for customer service that most people readily believe it.

What kind of reputation does your company have? Again, ask the question, "Would I buy from me or us?" Can you cite more than one customer horror story in your company? If so, you have your work cut out for you. Do everything you can for your customers. There's a vast difference, however, between doing everything you can for a customer and becoming a victim yourself.

Some customers will try to take advantage of you if they think you're an "easy mark." It's amazing to me how many people try to beat the system when they are dealing with a customer-centric company.

One of my favorite examples of customer service occurred when I was selling a bread machine on QVC back in the early 90's. Those were the halcyon days of that product. It was new, easy, fun, and made really good bread. I made it my business to find out everything I could about baking bread. I bought some cookbooks and made a trip to the library before the presentation. I read everything I could about the subject so I could effectively communicate the unit's benefits to our customers. I was ready.

Customer calls from satisfied users really helped to sell products on-air, and the bread machine was no exception. During my presentation, I took a phone call while adding the ingredients to the machine. However, it wasn't from a satisfied customer. "Steve," the customer said, "I bought that bread machine and I can't make bread in it to save my life." Immediately, the producer was asking me in my ear (via the receiver all hosts wear) if I wanted to dump the call. While I was off camera, I indicated "no."

I asked the caller to tell me everything she did when she baked a loaf of bread in the machine, which she began to do, in great detail. The producer kept me apprised of the fact that sales were dropping radically during the conversation. He kept urging me to drop the call and eventually said that my boss had called and really wanted us to drop the call. I was at the mercy of people in the control room, but figured that they'd stay with me until I paused long enough to allow them to "gracefully" dump out of the call. I didn't allow a moment of silence. This customer had bought the machine from us, and I was going to solve her problem or die trying. That's what a salesperson does.

I didn't catch anything wrong in her first run through, so I asked her to repeat the process. By now, there were executives in the studio, all frowning at the fact that I was "wasting" valuable airtime. The producer informed me that sales calls had dropped to almost zero. But this time the customer said, "I get the yeast out of the refrigerator..."

Bingo! That was it. Although I had known nothing about baking before presenting the machine, I had read that yeast is a living culture and must be kept in a cool, dry place—not cold, cool! She had obviously killed the yeast by placing it in the refrigerator. I told her that and reminded her that she could use our 30-day money back guarantee and send the machine back for a refund or give it another try with new yeast and then still send it back if it didn't work. She said she would try again.

The phones exploded. In the middle of a weekday afternoon, we sold more bread machines than anyone else up to that point in our history, regardless of time or day. And, we didn't exceed the time allotted for the presentation. Yes, I endured a bit of a chewing out for not following orders, but like many times in the past, my results kept me from the unemployment line. And I had the satisfaction that comes from providing excellent customer service. I did receive a letter from the customer telling me that my advice had worked, and she was now making great fresh bread for her family every day. Hey, we sold treadmills too.

When I started working for Shop At Home in Nashville, we initially sold most products on four or five stretch payments.

Before I arrived, the hosts used this stretch pay plan as a sales tool rather than a customer convenience. Their high-pressure sales presentations often included the phrase "...and just $99 gets it home." Yes it did, but you still had to make four more payments of $99 before you truly owned the product.

There were many people who were buying the product based on "$99 gets it home." When the next payments came due, their credit cards were often pegged and a quite protracted and expensive bad debt collection process ensued. Many other people were establishing phony accounts in order to get a computer for the first stretch payment and then "disappearing" before the next payments were due.

When I arrived, I immediately stopped the technique of selling an item based on stretch pay. Bad debt and product return rates decreased. Like me, you probably think that this type of scam is more work for a purchaser than getting a real job. It is amazing what lengths some people will go to beat the system, and get something for nothing. Most of your customers are fine, upstanding citizens. Still, be aware that there are always those who will try to take advantage of any situation. Train your people to know the difference. It will be money well spent.

"Would you buy from you?" "Would you do business with your company?" These have been two invaluable questions for me. When I started coaching the hosts at Shop At Home, many of them were like a high-pressure car salesperson. One of the first presentations I watched had the host and guest "threatening" the customer 19 times in two minutes that the product was going to sell out. It didn't ever sell out, but that didn't stop the next host/guest pairing from threatening the same scenario. But 19 times in two minutes was a record worthy of Guinness.

I got a lot of flack from most of the hosts when I explained to them that we weren't going to sell that way anymore. They had every right to be upset. Selling by intimidation works, but it is fraught with buyers' remorse. Shop At Home's returns were astronomical! As a Vice President, I had to pull rank more than a few times to get the hosts in line. It was a constant battle. While sales dropped at first, return rates dropped substantially.

Sales quickly increased as our customer base got accustomed to the new softer sales strategy.

I was surprised that before I got there none of the hosts had ever asked themselves the question, "Would I buy from me?" It made a difference and helped even the most stubborn long timer see that a true customer-centric way of selling was more effective in the long term.

It all goes back to the original "custom" meaning of the word *customer*. Truly successful companies realize that real customers are special and must be treated as such. During every phase of your customers' experience, they should feel that their needs are being completely met in every way. To wrap up, here are a few questions that will help you create a "custom" customer experience:

- Would I buy from me or us?
- Do we know who our customers are?
- Are our salespeople (myself included) addressing all of our customers' needs and concerns in their sales presentations?
- Is our ordering process "custom-made" for our customers?

- Are our salespeople and customer service personnel trained and empowered to quickly and efficiently solve any and all problems our customers may have?
- Do we have programs and procedures in place to make our customers feel like we know and appreciate them? Do we use these often?

It's not rocket science. Know your customers and then treat them that way. Make sure you would do business with you. It's a sure way to "customize" success.

The Oldest Profession...
No, It's Not What You're Thinking!

I remember hearing references to the "the oldest profession" on TV and radio shows in the 1950's and 60's. As a pre-teen, I didn't know what they referring to, so I asked the bastion of all knowledge, my mother. She delicately explained to me what the reference meant, but I still wasn't sure.

Eventually, when I reached my early teens in the mid-60's, it became clear. I snickered most times I thought about it. It wasn't until I entered the world of sales that I realized what "the oldest profession" really was.

You see, before that titillating occupation could be considered a profession, it had to be sold. Truly, the oldest profession is sales.

Think about it. Before Noah built the Ark, he had to be "sold" on the idea that the world was about to be destroyed. Before Lewis and Clark started off on their historic quest, the idea of the benefits of their trek had to be sold to the government. Whether your product is a commodity, service or an idea, selling is selling. This concept has served me well in every aspect of my life and career.

Throughout this book, you'll read about the value of breaking the paradigms that stifle creativity and productivity in today's business world as well as your personal life. Thinking of every aspect of your job as a sales opportunity will help you to do this. Here are some examples:

When I got my first job in advertising (as a writer, not a salesperson), I was put in an office with several other experienced writers all of whom had impressive talents and credentials. Before we would be assigned a job, we had to sell our ideas for a job to the Creative Director in what was called a pitch meeting. Citing their experiences and successes, the experienced writers made very effective presentations. In those early days, most times the veteran writers got the assignments, and I was assigned to them as an assistant.

While assistant sounds like a great position for newcomer, in essence I was a glorified gofer. While my skills at getting everyone's coffee and doughnuts order right were getting a workout, my creative juices were starting to dry up. When I was given the opportunity to pitch a new project, I spoke about the creativity and uniqueness of the idea, not the benefits to our client or the agency. My early failures at those pitch meetings made me realize that everything was a selling opportunity. Why would the powers-that-be choose me for an important advertising project when I couldn't even convince them I was the right person for the job?

At one pitch meeting for an important marketing film for a large high tech company, I applied the best of my sales abilities to my proposal. Having done a great deal of comedy writing while in radio, I wrote a humorous proposal. Instead of detailing a long and involved script for the company, I proposed the use of a comedic script; specifically a script that would use "music videos" of various song parodies to highlight the benefits of the company's new product.

The more experienced writers "stayed between the lines." They noted their track records and numerous awards they had won. One of them had even won a prestigious industry award for a similar type of film.

Their proposals were fraught with detail and historical precedents. Mine contained a few pages of suggested songs and videos to parody that would illustrate the benefits of the new product.

The owner of the ad agency carefully read and considered all the proposals. He then made a statement that I have never forgotten, "You can't eat awards." He went on to note that the safe course of action was to have one of his senior writers take on the project. He also said, "Not many people get rich playing it safe."

I got the assignment, but there was one problem. While I had written and produced a lot of song parodies for radio, I had never produced a music video, let alone a funny music video that would look and sound much like the original song being lampooned.

When I wrote the proposal for the project, I had to carefully research the production and talent costs for the film. They were sizable enough that I knew the proposal would have to be persuasive enough to offset the higher cost of the project. I had convinced my employers; I now had to convince the client.

In the proposal to my company, I had included a budget for producing a short music video to be used in the client proposal. I had even produced a short audio clip of the proposed parody. I was later told it was that detail that helped me to get the project in the first place.

The old adage "Be careful what you ask for, you might just get it" certainly applied here. I had never produced a music video before. Even though I had budgeted for an experienced video producer, the time demand was enormous. After several all-nighters, we finished the video for the client proposal.

I tried to hide my exhaustion at the client meeting. After going thorough the proposal, we showed our client the video. They loved it! They asked if we could produce the entire film in a month, less than half the proposed time. After we explained the inherent rush charges, they agreed.

It was the longest month of my life. Long days, late nights, all-nighters—it looked like it would never end. But it did. And the story has a very happy ending. The project was extremely successful for the client, so much so that just a few months after we finished, I was named Creative Director for the agency.

If you're doing it right, you're always selling. Whether it's in your business or personal life, your sales skills should be your greatest ally. I'm always amazed at the confrontations I see everyday that could be avoided if someone would make a convincing argument, not just an argument for argument's sake.

Recently, I was at a meeting where the company president and a senior executive had a serious disagreement. Both remained intransient as they stuck to their points of view. They were steadfast; each was convinced that his or her viewpoint represented the right course of action. What ensued was a fairly heated argument that went on for several minutes.

I'm no fan of long meetings and really frown on anything that makes a long meeting even longer. The discourse between these two executives became heated and increasingly more difficult to endure. Neither executive made a convincing case as to why his or her idea would benefit the company. Both stated their cases as they applied to and impacted them and them alone. No teamwork was evident.

It was a classic lose-lose scenario. Given their respective levels of success, surely both of these people had amassed substantial sales skills. But you wouldn't have known it from their diatribes. It was all "me, me, me." Eventually, the president announced that for the time being the subject was tabled. I almost applauded.

Had either of them made a convincing case for what his or her point of view meant to the company, the rest of us would have felt comfortable chiming in with possible solutions. Instead, we were treated to a verbal onslaught that resembled an aural version of the WWF. Both had forgotten their "first profession."

There are still times in my life, although not many I'm proud to say, when I forget that I'm a pretty good salesperson. One such incident was when I tried to convince QVC to bring in Tony Robbins. Many years ago, Tony's program had helped me to turn my life around. I was so excited that I went to the buyers and passionately made my case.

They were impressed enough to present it to the company president, who was not a Tony Robbins fan.

He turned it down; citing that the Tony Robbins system was "not appropriate for our customer." (I get to lampoon him and many others in the Chapter "But That's The Way We've Always Done It.") But the fact that we didn't start selling the Tony Robbins program wasn't totally the fault of our dogmatic president. It was mostly my fault.

You see, I was so passionate about the Tony Robbins program that I had stressed the benefits I had received rather than what QVC would receive if they offered it on the air. While I knew the sales would be tremendous, I spoke about the changes I had made in my life after taking the 30-day course. QVC is a retailer. They care about customer service and sales. The fact that the program had helped me get out of debt in a few months meant nothing to them.

About a year later, we got a new president and I decided to try my pitch again. While it wasn't the job of an on-air salesperson to source product, from time to time most of us would bring in items that interested us. I had a second chance and relied on my advertising background to structure the pitch to the buyers. This time I had researched sales figures for the Tony

Robbins program. They were quite impressive. In my presentation to the buyers, I stressed our company's income potential and just glossed over the impact the program had on my life.

The buyers made another similar presentation to the new president who agreed to give it a try. I was chosen to be the first host to work with Tony. Before we went on, I handed Tony a note asking him to read it when the show was finished. About half way through the one-hour show, we had sold out of all available product and the buyers had to scramble to find additional goods to sell. They did and the hour went on to gross well over a million dollars.

When we were finished, Tony took the note from his pocket and read it. I had written: "We will sell out of all the available product and the show will gross over $1,000,000." (I'm not psychic, just confident in my abilities as a salesperson.)

I realized that, before they would carry it, I had to stress the benefits of carrying the Tony Robbins program to QVC, namely sales and profit. During the presentation, I obviously used the benefits the audience would receive, i.e., the possibility of a better quality of life, happier relationships, better decisions, etc. But if I hadn't used my sales abilities to convince the company in the first place, Tony Robbins may have never come to QVC. His sales are in the tens of millions each year.

Having spent a few years doing various talk radio shows, I'm always surprised how many talk hosts don't try to sell their point of view in more effective ways. Most Liberal or Conservative hosts stick rigidly to their rather narrow points of view, stressing dogma rather than the benefits of their ideology.

One exception to this was Rush Limbaugh in his early years of national syndication. In those days, Rush would criticize politicians when he thought they deserved it and praise them the same way. He would back up his ideology with facts and logic and would even allow his opinions to be influenced by his callers.

Rush's style and commitment to his listeners changed the face and voice of talk radio forever. His pursuit of excellence was obvious to anyone who listened. He did an entertaining and informative show.

Even though I didn't often agree with him, I listened, as did millions, because I was entertained. He stressed the benefits of his beliefs and sometimes even got me to change my mind.

Rush spawned numerous imitators who went on to do extremely imperfect impressions of the original. Soon, the media began to group Limbaugh and his imitators together as "conservative talk radio." A movement, of sorts, was born.

As Limbaugh's show grew in popularity, he became more and more rigidly conservative. National politicians embraced him, and his show. The listener was treated to fewer thought provoking segments and more and more unbending Republican canons. Things progressed much the same way on the Liberal side. Inflexible views and marching orders quickly replaced creativity, thought-provoking commentary, and entertainment. I think there's a real opportunity for a creative radio personality to emerge from the cacophony of mindless doctrines. All it will take is a talk radio professional who remembers he or she has to sell their ideas to the audience in an entertaining manner.

Speaking of that, how many times have you tuned in your favorite radio station only to find out that they have changed format? Your favorite local talk station is now all syndicated sports; the classic rock station you loved is now *All Polkas, All the Time*. It seems to be happening more and more frequently these days.

Conventional wisdom says that when a station changes formats, they "stunt" for a few days. A stunt could be anything from playing the same song over and over for days or a simple countdown from 1,000,000 to 0, which also takes days. Radio experts believe that you will keep tuning in to find out what's happening.

It really makes me angry. Why don't they run an advertising and marketing campaign, selling you on why they are changing? Of course, the real reason they're dumping the old format is because their ratings and revenue are down.

It's interesting to note the case of a popular talk radio station in Philadelphia who did an hours-long on-air countdown prior to a major format change. Their new format died a few months later. Would an effective advertising and marketing campaign have made the new format more successful? While there's no way of knowing, it certainly would have eliminated all the bad press and negative news group and bulletin board posts.

Sell me on why this change is good for me as a listener. I might not buy it, but I surely wouldn't be as upset as I was when I tuned in and heard, "9,999, 9,998, 9,997..."

As you've seen in this chapter, regardless of our professions or personalities, while each of us is a salesperson, many of us don't use those sales skills when they could do us the most good. Think about your parents or your own parenting skills. "Because I'm your parent and I said so," seems to be a reasonable answer for most problems with your children, but it really represents a missed opportunity.

Remember the show "Leave It To Beaver?" The show featured the archetypical nuclear 50's family; a stay at home mom, professional dad and two average kids. Maybe, but something about the show always bothered me.

If you watch virtually any episode, you hear Beaver and Wally worrying about how their father is going to "kill them" for some minor transgression. They said it all the time, "Boy, Wally, Dad is going to kill us."

What kind of secret monster was Ward Cleaver? What horrors happened at 211 Pine Street? Seriously, regardless of the stupid and thoughtless things I did while growing up in the 50's and 60's, I never once thought a parent would kill me.

Long before it was the norm, my mom was a single parent in the 1950's and 1960's. While I had the influence of my Great Uncle Ed, she raised me pretty much single-handedly. She never threatened me. She was a great debater and used her substantial sales skills to guide me.

When I was "busted" by the authorities for having a pirate radio station, she sat me down and asked me why I had taken the time to build the transmitter and do a regularly scheduled show. There was no yelling, no threatening, just a logical series of questions to find out why I had flaunted federal law.

Once she found out that I did it because I loved radio and wanted to do a show, she suggested that I should contact the local radio stations and see if I could get an internship. As a teenager, I had never thought about doing it the conventional way. I did, and after some trial and error, I was working part-time at a local radio station, even doing a regular on-air report about the "news" at my local high school.

My mother sold me on the idea of following my dream. She also indicated that she was extremely disappointed that I had broken the law. I was facing thousands in fines and up to a year in jail. She told me she would stick with me during the impending hassles with the government and we would abide by their decisions. Luckily, I was just slapped on the wrist and told to go and sin no more.

If she had threatened or seriously punished me, my lifelong love affair with radio might never have happened. She didn't ignore the seriousness of my actions. Instead, she found out the root cause and urged me to go about things properly. She sold me on the idea of pursuing a goal in a positive and creative manner.

In fact, when I couldn't get into a radio station during regular business hours, she urged me to try to get in on the weekends, when a part-timer might be more willing to provide an impromptu tour. This proved to be the case.

How many parents have squashed the dreams of a child by forgetting that selling beats yelling every time? Can you imagine what Ward Cleaver would have done if the Beaver and Wally had been running a pirate radio station? I'll bet the cold case folks might be digging up a couple of teenage corpses someplace.

There are so many times in life where remembering to use your sales skills would make things so much better. I've shown examples in business and personal situations. When was the last time you could have improved things by selling your idea effectively?

How many times have you had a hassle with a relative, salesperson, or someone in customer service? I'll bet you engaged him or her in an argument, trying to desperately prove that you are right. All the while, the other person was doing exactly the same.

Did you ever consider trying to sell, rather than argue, your perspective? What are the benefits to them? What are the negatives?

Argue or sell? Once you realize we're all in "the oldest profession," the answer is pretty easy.

Bringing Your *A-Game*

The original Woodstock was an incredible event. Over 500,000 people witnessed dozens of bands and performers making complete fools of themselves.

Why such a harsh criticism? First of all, I was there. I really was and, unlike many attendees and musicians, I remember it. If you watch Michael Wadleigh's excellent documentary film, you'll get a pretty good idea of how simultaneously amazing and disappointing the event was.

Band after band took the stage so drunk and stoned that they made more mistakes than you'll hear at a local karaoke night. Even the Who, a band I've always enjoyed, were so apparently stoned that Roger Daltrey, their usually excellent singer, was often flat, and the band itself was completely disorganized.

"But Steve, it was the 60's, the age of sex, drugs and rock and roll. They were just staying true to the times."

What a load of crap! I was as much a part of the 60's as anyone. I saw a lot of bands perform stoned and/or drunk at much smaller venues, but not too drunk or stoned to serve their customers (the audience). Woodstock was graduation day. It was a chance to play for a social happening the likes of which will probably never be repeated. Woodstock made superstars out of some very unlikely musicians. These were the people who came with their A-Game. A few musicians and performers came to the festival ready to dazzle the half million attendees with everything they had.

Richie Havens opened the festival. He was a unique folk musician from the Greenwich Village scene. Using then-relatively-unknown open guitar tunings along with his distinctive voice, he was wowing audiences at small folk clubs around New York. He was hired as an opening act for the many superstars who were booked. If not for fact that he brought his A-Game, he probably wouldn't have made it to the final cut of the documentary film.

Woodstock attracted several hundred thousand more attendees than expected. In true 60's style, most of these extra attendees hadn't bought tickets. "New State Thruway's closed, man," Arlo Guthrie announced to the audience. He was right. The crush of unexpected traffic virtually gridlocked all of upstate New York. Even performers couldn't make it to the venue.

Richie performed Friday afternoon, before any other performers had arrived. While concert promoters were arranging helicopters to bring in other performers, they continued to extend Richie's performance, which was originally slated to be a half-hour. Every time he got up to leave the stage, the promoters motioned to him to continue playing. He played for almost three hours... three unforgettable hours!

He had obviously brought his A-Game to Woodstock. Even his last song, "Freedom," was phenomenal, especially considering that, after three hours, he was out of material and made it up on the spot. It was so good that it became one of the anthems of the event as well as the era. It was prominently featured in the film and soundtrack.

Richie Havens was fantastic! This one man with an acoustic guitar, backed by another guitar and conga drums, held over 500,000 people in the palm of his hand for three hours...and we still wanted more.

Without a doubt, he brought his A-Game. After Woodstock, he began to play much larger venues and receive major national attention. He soon appeared on *The Tonight Show with Johnny Carson* and became the only performer in the show's history (right through today) who received a 10-minute standing ovation. It was so long that they had to edit the tape before it aired so the show wouldn't run overtime.

I'm sure a lot of performers, especially those who were already superstars, saw Woodstock as one huge party. They decided to live it up. Most were young, and no one was telling them what to do. Richie Havens was young, too. As young as he was, he saw Woodstock as fantastic opportunity to showcase his A-Game. If he partied hearty, it was obviously after his performance. To this day, every time I've seen him, he gives his audience quite a show.

The band Ten Years After also brought their A-Game to the Woodstock festivities. Led by guitar virtuoso Alvin Lee, Ten Years After was a British club band who had released a few LPs and was getting some FM airplay. They brought their A-Game to Woodstock, finishing their set with a 10 minute-plus version of "Going

Home," which became a huge FM hit, and was one of the standout moments of the festival and the subsequent Wadleigh film.

Like Richie Havens, Ten Years After's career exploded after Woodstock. They became headliners, regularly selling out major venues around the country. And while they never equaled their live or recorded Woodstock success, by bringing their A-Game to "the world's biggest party," they ensured their place in rock and roll history.

While some of the bands who didn't bring their A-Game to Woodstock went on to have fine careers, the popularity of Havens and Ten Years After increased exponentially after the festival. Who knows what would have happened if some of the other so-called superstars had brought their A-Game and made the festival about their customers (fans) instead of their own good times.

It's easy to recognize the people in the world of sports who always bring their A-Game. Whether it's for the love of the game or the huge salaries and bonuses, most pro athletes bring their A-Game almost every day.

When they don't, the results are painfully obvious. Anything from a one-sided blowout to a bench-clearing brawl can usually be traced back to people not bringing their A-Game.

As a salesperson, do you always bring your A-Game? Or, depending on the client, project, or event, do you sometimes attempt to slip by with less than your personal best? What's been the outcome? Did you get the result you wanted, or did you get the one you deserved?

In my advertising days, I remember writing and producing a film for a small, non-profit organization. It was a low-budget affair and, as was usually the case with low budget projects, the client wanted an A+ production. Everyone at the agency was working on several large active projects at the time, and we were less than enthusiastic that another "less important" task had been added to our plates.

During the pre-production meetings, there was a lot of talk about doing just enough to satisfy the client. Without much hassle, we could have thrown together a film that would be okay.

It probably would have made the client happy. We even put together a storyboard for the project, which the client really liked.

We watched the first animated sequence and all of us were less than pleased. It looked cheesy. Our agency was known for producing first class material, and our client list read like a Who's Who of American business: AT&T, Southern Bell, IBM, Coke and many Fortune 500 Companies trusted us with some of their most important advertising and marketing projects. Our work for them was always cutting-edge, state-of-the-art; as good as we could make it. The same people who produced that caliber of work were now looking at something none of us would have submitted as a college project.

We decided to redo the opening sequence and then made sure the rest of the film was up to our personal and professional standards. We even created an original song for the film and found a way to produce it without blowing the little film's budget. Needless to say, the client was delighted and so were we. It was a great little film that really did the job for the non-profit agency.

Their contributions soared and we got a little good press out of it. But the benefits of bringing our A-Game to the project didn't end there.

It seems that a member of their board was a major executive at large entertainment company. He was so impressed with our work that he commissioned us to create a musical show for a major amusement park. Our original song for the little film had convinced him that we were the go-to company for this type of project. Up until then, our company was not known for original music. We hired the best composer in town and created a great show.

This new project succeeded beyond our wildest expectations. We became one of the top agencies in town for original music, which proved to be a really profitable enterprise. And it all came from a little film that we almost overlooked. Since that time, I have tried to bring my A-Game to every project I've done. When I think back on my career and the times I didn't bring my A-Game, I wonder how many opportunities I've missed.

I have to admit, during my 15-year tenure at QVC,

there were few times when I didn't bring my A-Game. One of those times was during a jewelry show. While jewelry was and is a mainstay of televised retailing, it was not my strong suite; I was most effective in technology, cooking and music shows. I did fine when I hosted a jewelry show, as long as the products were good. One day, the products were horrid, in my opinion. It seemed like they had put every ugly, poor-selling piece of jewelry into one hour.

Rather than bringing my A-Game to the show, I decided to use the hour as an excuse to promote all my upcoming shows. If I had been a customer looking for a piece of jewelry, I would have turned off the show in a New York minute. I watched the tape and was truly embarrassed at my performance...or lack thereof.

But my embarrassment was just the beginning. Even though I was one of QVC's top-producing hosts, I was put on probation and taken off all jewelry shows until I completed an in-house training program. For the next few weeks, it was very embarrassing to face my peers. Human nature being what it is, many of them were pleased that I had been "taken down a notch."

This was a lesson I never forgot. After completing my probationary period and training, I decided to continue my jewelry education, taking the highly regarded Gemological Institute of America (GIA) course. My jewelry numbers took a quantum leap. When I was sent to England to train the hosts on QVC UK, I was able to bring my A-Game to jewelry training as well as technology and cooking. In fact, using the opportunity to teach by example, I was the first host on QVC UK to host a major successful jewelry show.

Over the years, I had the opportunity to work with many celebrities and professionals who were known for their A-Game and some who were not. One of the former was Jeanne Bice, the innovative entrepreneur behind the phenomenal success of Quacker Factory fashions. If you've never seen a piece of fashion from Quacker Factory, it's difficult to describe. It's whimsical, fun and fashionable all at the same time, combining lots of embroidery and appliqué along with great fabrics.

I was the first host to work with Jeanne on QVC. She was very open about the fact that, since she was designing women's fashion, she wanted to work with a woman.

QVC was steadfast about their host choice and she was stuck with me. What she didn't know is that I took the time necessary to learn as much about women's fashion as I could before the show. As a result, we sold out her original blouse in a few minutes.

She has parlayed that success into a multi-million dollar fashion empire. To this day, she not only brings her A-Game on-air, Jeanne brings it to every aspect of her business. She stays current with emerging trends and fads, always offering her customer something new and exciting. Her fashions are so popular that she could rest on her laurels and simply update her most popular sellers. But you can tell from her upbeat on-air demeanor that she won't ever settle for second best.

There's an interesting side note about Jeanne Bice. She once did a show that generated tens of thousands of orders in two hours. Of those orders, fewer than a dozen were from new customers. When a QVC executive asked me what we could do about it, I replied, "Hire her. She obviously knows exactly what our customers want." While new products are the "life's blood" of any retailer, we had many other product lines that generated lots of new customers.

I am so pleased that she continues to thrive at QVC. She is a wonderful person and really cares about her customers.

How about you? I know it might seem like motivational claptrap, but are you bringing your A-Game to all aspects of the sales process? Yes? Good, but how about after the sale? (For more about that, check out the chapter on Customer Communication.)

For more examples of people who always bring their A-Game, look at successful people in any endeavor. You won't find two more divergent personalities than Howard Stern and Rush Limbaugh. Both host extremely popular radio shows. Why are their shows so successful? Are they known for showing up ten minutes before their shows? Do they take weekends off, never once doing or thinking about anything involving their shows? Are they penny-wise and pound-foolish when it comes to their staff and the elements of their shows? "Of course not" is the answer to the last three questions.

Both Howard and Rush work long hours. I can hear some of the responses now; "Yeah, but do you see how much money they make? I'd work that hard if I made that much." Do you think they always made that much money? No! Did they always work as hard as they do now, even when they were making a pittance? Yes! That's why their shows succeeded and why they're making so much money now.

When you service a small account, do you give it as much time as a large account? Do you spend some of your off time figuring out ways to be more successful? Do you ever invest in yourself and your success without expecting your company to reimburse you? I hope there was at least one "yes" answer to those questions. If you gave three "yes" answers, then you're well on your road to success.

When I moved to Nashville, one of the most cumbersome things I had to move was my book collection. I have over 3000 hardbound books, most dealing with sales, success and related fields. I never asked my employer to reimburse me for any of them. I considered them a CTDB, Cost To Do Business.

Let me ask you a quick question. What (and when) was the last sales or business-related book you read? If you had to go back more than a year for your answer, I suspect things aren't going the way you'd like right now. How about the last sales seminar you attended? Oh, I see; the company wouldn't pay for it, so you didn't go. Recently, Ron Maestri, I host I hired at the Shop at Home Network, and I attended a major industry seminar at our own expense. It should come as no surprise that Ron was one of the top-selling hosts of Shop At Home. Not only did he do his homework, he wasn't afraid to pay for it. He is a perfect example of someone who always brings his or her A-Game.

Bringing your A-Game isn't just about your performance; it's about your preparation. What kind of research do you do before calling on a client? If you just check the Business Phone Directory to see how many competing businesses there are, again, I imagine your lot in life at this moment leaves something to be desired.

When I first arrived at Shop At Home, I asked one of their top show hosts what kind of research he did before a show.

He proudly announced he did a great deal of comparison-shopping to make sure we had the lowest prices available on the products he sold. When I asked him if he researched industry trends for the products he was presenting, he looked at me like I was speaking a foreign language. It took some time, but I was able to convince most of the on-air sales staff of Shop At Home that sales aren't made on price or savings alone.

If you're selling on price alone, you're doomed. Get out of whatever business you're in and find another career! Wal-Mart sells very successfully on price. Everyone else in retail who tries to emulate this tactic gets killed by this merchandising giant. Regardless of your customers or products, the moment you start selling them on price alone you have made your products a commodity, one that can be easily outbid if the competition is willing to take a smaller margin.

Bringing your A-Game extends to all aspects of your sales process; the preparation, the sales process itself, service-after-the-sale and anything else that serves your customer. Let me repeat that last line: "Anything else that serves your customer."

Although that's a wide-open category, it's a crucial part of bringing your A-Game to the sale. You must be willing to serve your customer any way that's required. Howard Stern and Rush Limbaugh do it. I do it. Any successful salesperson or company does it as well. Do you listen to your customer, especially after the sale? Or, are you like the stereo store employee (I won't call him a salesperson) I referred to in the Customer Service chapter?

In the world of basketball, did Michael Jordan just work out, practice, and show up at games? No, he communicated with his fans and even hired several people to help him do it. I once saw him sign an autograph for a young fan while he was having dinner. He smiled, signed the autograph, spoke to the young man for a few moments and then turned his attention back to his dinner guests. He was a gentleman on and off the court. One of the reasons he's a legend is that his A-Game extended to every aspect of his career.

Speaking of sports, I remember my older brother Jack (God rest his soul) taking me to a Phillies game at the old Connie Mack stadium in Philadelphia when I was 11 or 12.

I caught a foul ball and we waited at the player's entrance after the game to get it signed. Every player who came out happily signed the ball, spoke with me and made me glad to be a Phillies' "customer." I wonder how many of today's baseball players would take the time to do that?

Baseball viewership and attendance continue to decline. Thanks to steroids, they can't blame it on the lack of home runs. Few players today bring their A-Game to their customers. They think it's enough to hit "long balls" and win games. If you want their autograph or even a few polite words, you'd better have your checkbook or credit card ready. It makes me want to go to a game or watch on TV, how about you?

Bring your A-Game to every aspect of the sales process. Find ways to refine it and make it better. It's hard work, but if you weren't born into money, it's the only way I know to achieve sustainable success.

Customer Communication

If your customers only hear from you when you send them an invoice, how could you afford to buy this book? You can't be making money as a salesperson. Ongoing, positive customer communication is vital to your success! If you don't regularly communicate with your customers, rest assured that someone else will—oh, and by the way, when that happens they won't be **your** customers anymore.

My experiences with positive customer communication date back to my advertising days. As the upstart agency in Atlanta, and a bunch of "Yankees" to boot, we had to overcome a lot of prejudice. One way we did it was by establishing a regular audio newsletter for current and prospective customers. We used song and commercial parodies, humor (edgy, but not offensive), current events along with advertising tips, and we interspersed them with commercials about our agency.

A real commercial would follow a well-produced parody spot, pointing out the state-of-the-art techniques we used for the spoof.

It worked better than even we expected. We grew very fast in those days and many new jobs and customers came from those audio newsletters. And notice that I used the word *customer* instead of *clients*. I always have. It's a nuance difference to be sure, but it has really helped me in my sales career. To me, the word *client* seems a bit detached. I wonder how the medical and legal profession would fare if they treated their clients and patients as customers? As long as they are regularly patronizing and recommending the attorney or physician, that's exactly what they are.

Today, an audio newsletter could be produced and distributed as a podcast. Your company would look very cutting edge to your customers. Salespeople could use the podcast to drive prospective clients to your website. Do it right. If you can't do it yourself, have it professionally produced. If you have a musician or computer wiz on staff with the proper equipment to produce it, work out a win-win intrapreneurial arrangement for him or her to do it.

If you do a quick brainstorming session, where you write down all your thoughts on a specific subject for five to ten minutes, you'll come up with at least one powerful idea about customer communication, probably many more. To get you in the mood, let me give you some more examples of customer communication from my experiences and observations over the years.

I love the guitar, especially acoustic guitars. In the course of doing research on my hobby, I learned that back in the 1920's, a German piano maker named Hermann C. Weissenborn immigrated to New York and began to make hollow neck guitars in response to the growing popularity of Hawaiian music. These instruments had greater volume and better tone for this type of music. I really wanted one of the original Weissenborns until I saw the work of Luther Bill Hardin, the owner of Bear Creek Guitars (www.bcguitar.com). Bill made reproductions that were reported to be as nice, if not better, than the originals.

I contacted Bill and he designed a perfect guitar for me. I made the down payment and waited, somewhat patiently, for the few months it would take to complete the instrument. A few days after I made the down payment, Bill sent me photos of the beginning stages of my guitar being built. I was thrilled. He regularly sent photos of my guitar as a work in progress. I felt very special as a customer.

When the guitar finally arrived, it was better than I had expected, and I had expected a lot. The same day it arrived, Bill called me to see if I liked it. We had a great conversation and Bill had a customer for life. The extra effort he took by sending me the construction photos meant almost as much as the exquisite workmanship on the guitar itself.

If you are in a craft, building or construction business, do you keep your customer updated like this? If not, start now. Through the years, I have recommended Bill to many other guitar enthusiasts. Whether or not these recommendations have resulted in a sale, he has always taken the time to thank me. How much more business could you generate from this type of customer communication?

People laugh when I tell them my wife and I bought our current house on the Internet, but it's true. When Shop At Home hired me, they wanted me in Nashville ASAP, so quickly that I didn't have time to fly down to find a home. My wife and I did some research on the Internet and found a great realtor. Margaret Frazier was a sales superstar with Shirley Zeitlin and Company Realtors in Nashville. We told her what we did and didn't want in a new house and she set out with her MLS listings and digital camera.

In a few days, we had comprehensive digital photos of many properties that met our criteria. Margaret even went back to a few of the houses and took specific photos. Her photos and information were so comprehensive that we made our decision and bought the house without a personal visit. Margaret had guided us every step of the way. It was the easiest transaction I've ever experienced.

It's interesting that a great salesperson like Margaret can transform the largest purchase most of us will ever make into such an enjoyable and successful experience. I know several car salespeople who could learn a lot from her.

After the sale, she even took us on a tour of our new hometown. She also gave us a great gift, a huge (and very expensive) onyx serving platter that we use regularly and really enjoy. How many times have you received a lousy thank you gift? Of course, that's why re-gifting a was invented.

We love this house! Thanks to Margaret's hard work, it's everything we wanted and a lot more. Because of her extraordinary service and communication, I have recommended her many times.

I've already told you about taking the time to answer my customers' email at QVC. In addition to this, I also made myself very available for speaking engagements. These weren't the $10,000 a pop, play for pay engagements that have made many people rich. (However, I wouldn't turn one of those down.) No, these were times when customers asked me to speak to their company or group. I jumped at the chance. Why? Well it wasn't for totally altruistic reasons.

I always enjoy giving my customers a little *lagniappe*, which is a Cajun term meaning "a little something extra." But, as an author, I have to believe the success of both my previous books was due in part to purchases and recommendations made by some of the people for whom I had done something extra. Get the idea? How could you adapt this idea to your career and/or life? When you do, the benefits will last a long time.

In my book *Sales Magic*, ©1993, Amherst Media (a bit more self-promotion never hurts), I wrote about the power of establishing yourself as an expert. Along with the goodwill generated by lecturing and teaching, engaging in activities like this also positions you as an expert. I did a great many pro bono presentations on camcorders and photography when I was writing my first book *Basic Camcorder Guide*, ©1989, 1991 Amherst Media. It sold very well in the early 1990's. It was so successful that I wrote a second updated edition a few years later, again giving lectures and seminars for free.

How much impact did the book have? Over 15 years later, I still receive many emails, especially around Christmastime, from people wanting camcorder recommendations. I still take the time to answer these requests. In fact, I get quite a kick out of it, and you never know when I might want to write another camcorder or photographic book.

I'm convinced that my many speaking engagements and the resultant word-of-mouth advertising added to the success of *Basic Camcorder Guide*. I did a lot of speaking engagements about sales and marketing when I was writing *Sales Magic*, which also sold very well. Coincidence? I know better.

Take some time and think about the people and companies with whom you do business. How do they communicate with you? Do they ever initiate communication? By the way, throwing a pamphlet wrapped in plastic on your driveway every day for a month doesn't count. I had a landscaper do that to me when I was desperately looking for one. Guess when he'll get my business? (Hint: Pigs will be flying and sweaters will be selling in Hades.)

Positive communication with your customers is vital. How many calls have you received from a car salesperson (sorry to pick on them, but there are a lot of really bad ones), trying to get you to buy a car. My favorite quote from that call is "What can I do to get you in this car today?" I always answer, "Stop calling me. If I decide I want the car, I'll call you."

Okay, how many calls have you received from a car salesperson after you buy a car? If he or she is any good at all, you should have answered, "Several." Even when I bought a car that cost more than my first house, I received just one call after the sale, "How do you like the car?" That's all the salesperson asked me. When will these people learn? Hey, they might be reading this book. If that's the case and you're that car salesperson, get ready to leave the competition in the dust.

If the salesperson who sold me that "mid-life crisis car" had communicated with me in any way other than service reminders, I might have gone back for another one. I didn't and now I drive a much more sensible vehicle. I figure that car salesperson lost a bundle in future commissions by not communicating with me. For the record, I loved the car and would have bought another one if the salesperson hadn't made me feel like my sale didn't matter. I wonder what he's doing now?

Communication can take many forms. Emails are nice, but very common these days. I always give a hard copy express delivery letter much more credence than an email. I have noticed that the order of impact, from lowest to highest, seems to be: direct mail, email, hard copy letter, and personal phone call. Notice that's "*personal* phone call." Ever get one of those calls from an automated calling machine? Other than hanging up the phone, did it make you take any action? Me neither.

There are examples of good and bad customer communication all around us. Even after I left QVC, I remained a customer. When I place an order, whether I speak to a live operator or use their automated ordering service, it's a very easy process. Immediately after placing my order, I receive a confirming email. I also receive an email letting me know when my order has been shipped. Even much smaller companies I deal with are this thorough. The people at ellusinoist.com are designers and sellers of magic products and videos. And while they're a much smaller company than QVC, you wouldn't know it from their customer communication. They provide almost the exact type of interaction as QVC. Because of this, they get the bulk of my business as a sleight-of-hand hobbyist. I also regularly recommend them to other magicians I meet. Guess that makes me a customer in the truest sense.

I also occasionally buy items from HSN, Home Shopping Network. I recently bought an electric wok because the demo really impressed me. I used their automated ordering process, which I will never do again. Even if the phones are busy and there is no other way to buy, I'd rather do without the item than go through that process again. Here's how it went:

It was fairly easy to use the touchtone keypad to place the order with HSN, but I find QVC's system to be a bit easier. Then it started. Automated upsells: "To get the maximum enjoyment from your new purchase, our chef recommends that you also purchase his gourmet sauces. To purchase them, press 1." I immediately pressed 2. "Our chef also recommends that you purchase his gourmet seasonings…." I pressed 2 again. "To add our chef's newest cookbook to your purchase, press…." I hit 2 again. This nonsense went on so long that I considered canceling the original purchase.

I understand the profitability of upsell items. The success of the Scion line of motor vehicles is based on add-ons, which often double the price of a $17,000 vehicle. But when you just want a wok, you shouldn't be bombarded with an almost endless stream of upsells. Make it optional: "To hear about ways to get more enjoyment from your new wok, press 1. To complete the sale, press 2."

For the record, to the best of my knowledge, QVC has rarely offered upsell items. QVC is almost a $7 billion dollar company. HSN is less than half that, and HSN started first, predating QVC by many years. Simply put, lousy customer communication is much worse than no communication at all. For the record, many direct response companies' reward their phone representatives for selling additional merchandise to their customers. The majority of the most successful companies do not.

Truth is vital to all customer communication. Starting at the sales process, if any of your customer communication is untruthful, start practicing, "Would you like fries with that?" Lying or exaggerating to your customer is worse than not communicating at all. "But, Steve, isn't most advertising based on exaggeration?" A lot of it used to be and, unfortunately, some of it still is. Thanks to crackdowns from the FTC, FDA, and other regulatory agencies, truth in advertising has become the rule and not the exception.

I'm proud to say that during my eight years in advertising I always insisted on telling the truth in our agency's ads. And I'm also proud to say that it didn't affect our business or our customer's sales. Sometimes it wasn't easy to convince a customer that hyperbole is not a valid advertising tool, but we did it.

There's a very sad story about a Subaru ad that touted the fact that the car had 63 safety features. When questioned about the source of the claim, the ad agency copywriter said he simply made it up. His defense was the fact that all advertising is based on exaggeration. Calling a claim like that "exaggeration" is like calling World War II a minor skirmish. The ad was pulled, but I wonder how many people still think that their Subaru has 63 different safety features? To their credit, Subaru has made a valiant effort to counteract this false claim.

A company can send a very powerful positive message to its customers when it honestly and openly admits to a mistake. Jackie Gleason hosted a game show back in 1961 called *You're in the Picture*. It was a very silly game show where celebrity contestants stuck their heads through a life-sized picture and asked Gleason questions to find out who they were. It was so bad that Gleason came back the next week, alone on a bare stage, and apologized about how bad the previous week had been.

His apology was such a smashing success that CBS had him host a regular weekly show where he would interview celebrities on the same type of minimalist stage. While this show only lasted a few months, it allowed customers (viewers) to see Jackie Gleason as their advocate. Jackie Gleason is widely regarded as a "regular guy" who was a brilliant entertainer. His honest communication back in 1961 on live, national TV certainly helped to solidify his image as a superstar.

My first experience with bad customer communication came in the mid-1950's. I used to get up early every Saturday morning and watch a show called *Space Patrol*. Back then I couldn't get enough of space and science fiction TV shows and movies. I still can't.

One Saturday morning I tuned in and *Space Patrol* was gone, replaced by an old western movie. It was the same the next Saturday morning. I finally asked my mother what had happened. She said she didn't know, but she took the time to write a note to the TV station to find out what had happened. About a month later, they sent her a brief, unsigned typewritten response telling her that *Space Patrol* had been cancelled. No other explanation was given.

This was 50 years ago, and I still remember being disappointed that the show was gone. Would things have been better for me (and all their customers) if the station had explained what happened on the first Saturday morning the show was gone? Absolutely! Even as a child, I could have understood that the show was gone. And I would have moved on with my life, as much as any five-year-old could. By dragging it out for weeks, they only prolonged the agony for their young fans. When the show returned a few years later (in reruns), remembering my previous disappointment, I didn't watch.

It was certainly a trivial occurrence in my life, but not trivial enough to forget. And why didn't they tell the truth and announce that the show had been cancelled in the first place? There's an entire chapter in this book all about that: "But That's the Way We've Always Done It."

Have you or your company ever publicly admitted to a mistake or flaw to your customers? Consider this: Volkswagen used a series of ads for its Beetle that acknowledged how "ugly" it was. Using lines like "beauty is only skin deep," along with many others, Volkswagen positioned itself as a solid, reliable, and fun car to the maturing Woodstock generation. The ads and the car were a success.

Looks like Volkswagen is poised to repeat the success of their "truth in advertising" strategy. Recent ads depicting staged crashes to prove the safety of the Volkswagen Jetta are extremely controversial. Yet, by acknowledging the fact that vehicles sometimes collide and that structural integrity is a key factor in vehicle safety, they've created a growing positive buzz. The ads end with a clear view of the crash damage.

Listerine had a series of ads a while ago that said, "Use Listerine and have fewer colds, milder colds." The problem is that a virus causes colds, and all viruses are invulnerable to antiseptics like Listerine. After repeated complaints from doctors and other medical practitioners, the FTC ordered Listerine to spend millions on ads to counteract this false claim that had been made for years. Listerine complied, but the ads seemed very insincere to me. The disclaimer was placed at the end of the ad and was treated like an afterthought. Although Listerine is successful today, I still won't use it. I won't use a product from a company that lied to me and then made a halfhearted apology. How much more business would Listerine have today if they had openly stated the truth and apologized to their customers? Like many, that figure is lost to the ages.

Many of the salespeople I've met that insist on making untruthful claims about their products seem to be cut from the same mold. How many people do you know who are never wrong, or at least never admit to being wrong? Like me, probably far too many. These "I'm always right" folks (I fought the urge to type *idiots*) seem to be the biggest offenders of lying to their customers.

Televised retailing is a great microcosm of these people. Watch any infomercial or televised shopping channel. The "I'm always right" people constantly yell, threaten their customers ("This is going to sell out!!!), and generally exaggerate a product's capabilities and the buyer's savings.

These traits are pretty universal, either in the office or just about anywhere in life. How many of these people do you run into every day? Hopefully they don't work for your company.

Today, many companies are very concerned with their internal communications, so much so that they neglect their customer communication. While it's important that the systems and processes in your company run smoothly, that smoothness should not be at the expense of customer communication. Whether it's via podcast, e-mail, hard copy delivery, CD or any other medium, make sure you regularly communicate with your customers. Make sure he or she feels like the most important person in the world to you and your company. They are!

Communicate truthfully with your customer every chance you get. Hyperbole might get you one buyer, but truthful, ongoing communication will help to build an army of true customers.

Be an Eternal Student

What was the title of the last sales book you read? When and where was the last sales seminar you attended? Have you searched the Internet lately for new sales ideas or product information? If you answered *no* to all three questions, maybe you can still get your money back for this book, because you're not dedicated to improving your skills, which means you're not really a salesperson.

However, if this is a first step in your rededication to your personal and professional growth, welcome! Don't return the book. You and I will both make out better if you keep it. This chapter will help you understand the reasons a true professional in any field is never finished studying and perfecting his or her craft...especially salespeople.

I can find great sales lessons in everyday life, movies, TV, radio shows, newspapers, and just about anything else. Someday, I'm going to write a book titled *Everything I Learned About Sales I learned from Star Trek.* Just about every character in all the different incarnations of the *Star Trek* franchise was a phenomenal salesperson. If you doubt that, watch one of the original episodes from the 1960's. Scottie had all of Starfleet convinced that he was the greatest engineer in the universe. Would a great engineer always be telling his commanding officer, "Captain, my engines cannot take it?" But I digress.

I have read at least one sales book per month for the past 15 years. I bought most of them, and I am very proud of my sales book library. A lot of salespeople ask me how many books they should read for their particular career. While I'm tempted to say something like, "How should I know?" I take the high road and reply, "How many do you think you should read?" That's the question I'm posing to you. How many sales books do you think you should read?

I choose to read one per month because it fits into my schedule. My sales numbers show that it must be working for me. Start reading today and you'll quickly find out what works for you. (Hint: One per month is not a huge drain on my personal time.)

So which books should you read? In a previous chapter, I've already mentioned Joe Girard's books. He's incredible! Additionally, add the books from Brian Tracy, Mary Kay Ash, Zig Ziegler, Tom Hopkins, Al Reis and Jack Trout to your list. These people redefined the sales process and achieved phenomenal success while doing it.

Even if a book starts off with the basics that you think you already know very well, don't gloss over them. The basics of the sales process, Features, Advantages and Benefits, etc, have to be automatic. Without a firm understanding of the building blocks of our craft, it's impossible to add the advanced techniques and nuances necessary to create compelling sales presentations.

By way of illustration, John Wooden was the coach of the UCLA basketball program for many years...many extremely successful years for the team. While his coaching experience and expertise are seemingly limitless, his dedication to the basics of the game is often credited with the many winning teams he coached.

Even when a high school superstar joined his team, Coach Wooden made him practice lay-ups, free throws and other basic skills for several weeks before allowing him to play in a scrimmage. He believed that the basics of any discipline must be automatic. He told his players that once they could perform the basic moves automatically, without even thinking about them, they were ready to play real basketball.

Along with the authors I've listed, there are thousands of other authors who have written excellent sales and marketing books. Rather than list them all, let me show you a technique that will help you to identify whether or not a book will help with your personal growth.

Next time you pick up a sales book, turn to any page at random and read for about 30 seconds. Do this three times. If you don't know something new after the third time, step away from the book. It won't help you. While this isn't a hard and fast rule, it hasn't let me down so far.

Sometimes you can judge a book by its cover. Many times when I pick up a sales book because I was initially attracted to the design of the cover, it passes the 30-second test with flying colors. I don't exactly know why, but I have a theory: If an author and publisher care enough to make their book's cover design stand out from the pack, they probably care just as much about the content. Happy reading!

Sales seminars are very tricky. Most are either great or awful. There are a lot of people who will tell you that even if you get just one great idea from a lousy seminar, you got your money's worth. Taken to its logical conclusion, that means if you buy a box of cookies and all but one are moldy, you win!

I've never subscribed to the "one great idea" theory. If I pay hundreds or thousands of dollars for a seminar, sacrificing days out of my schedule to attend, I better come out with more ideas than I could ever use. That's easy to say, but separating the wheat from the crap in sales seminars is much more involved than finding a good sales book.

Try to find some people who attended a previous session of the seminar you're considering. Any reputable speaker or sales organization should have a list of contacts. Call these people, but don't stop there.

There is a chance that they are being compensated in some way for their glowing words. Once, (and just once, thankfully) I attended a seminar after calling one person on the suggested list. Her words were so glowing that I thought I couldn't miss. I was wrong. It was one of the worst seminars I've ever attended. I didn't know it, but the lady I called was the speaker's sister-in-law. She wanted to make sure her sister's husband remained gainfully employed. Lesson learned.

Now when I consider attending a seminar, I use my sales network to find someone who's not on the suggested list of previous attendees. It usually works, saving me a lot of time, money and aggravation.

In the rare cases when I can't find an unbiased testimonial, I rely on my gut. Who is leading the seminar? Have I read his or her books? Did I like them? Does the time allotted for the seminar seem sufficient for the material that's going to be covered? (It could be too short or too long.) If I come up with positive answers to these questions, I'm off to the seminar. If not, I assuage my disappointment with a trip to the bookstore for a new sales tome.

Sometimes a seminar will seem too good to be true. For instance, I attended a one-day event in Philadelphia where several of my sales heroes were going to speak. I couldn't believe that it only cost $49.99. As a direct response salesperson, the price should have been my first clue.

True to the advertising, over a half dozen of the leading sales and motivational experts in the country spoke. Each gave a stirring talk for a few minutes, followed by a lengthy sales pitch for their "advanced" sales and motivational materials. Most of these book and CD sets sold for $300 or more. As speaker after speaker did exactly the same pitch, I felt betrayed. By the end of the day, I was a bit disillusioned. Since that day, I haven't recommended any books or seminars by these people, and I probably never will. It's interesting to note that I never received any replies to the letters I wrote to some of the speakers, expressing my disappointment.

Another great way to continue learning your craft is to join a trade association. Like seminars, some are great, some stink, and some don't exist at all. If the latter is the case, maybe you could start one.

Deciding which trade association(s) to join is just a tricky as finding a good seminar. You can always ask a member. Unfortunately, that's a lot like asking a seminar attendee for an opinion. You never know when someone's personal agenda will preclude an honest appraisal.

When I want to find out about trade associations, I check the Internet for articles and press releases. Within a few minutes, I usually find out the real story. This way I can find out the names of the key members and do some searches on them. What did we do before the Internet? Remember microfiche at the library? I don't miss those days one tiny bit.

In the event that a trade association doesn't exist, consider starting one. Realize that, outside of medical school, it will be the biggest drain on your time you've ever experienced. Still, the benefits of being able to learn and share ideas with your peers can be extremely valuable. Believe it or not, there is no major trade association for televised shopping channels. I am seriously considering starting one. Hey, I can always take that vacation in 2017.

Do you regularly see sales lessons in the media? I do. I've already mentioned *Star Trek*, albeit somewhat tongue-in-cheek. But there are great sales lessons that can be learned from non-sales books and magazines, radio and TV shows, and movies. For TV, radio, and movies, don't just concentrate on the content, although that can be valuable as well. Examine the ways in which these media promote and schedule their programming, and you'll find a never-ending stream of sales messages. Once you identify them, it's an easy task to modify them and then model them in you discipline. Here are some examples:

Terrestrial radio (AM and FM) has made enough mistakes in the past few decades to fill a set of encyclopedias, maybe two. Take the example of the *Jack* format. Radio is very big on the monosyllabic names for their "new and improved" formats. *Jack* plays the greatest hits from several decades. Their slogan is "*Jack,* playing what ***we*** want." Great! I feel special as a listener, how about you?

The strategy was to make them sound like rebels, trying to invoke the spirit of 60's' freeform radio to aging Baby Boomers. What a colossal waste of airspace! Oh, to have been a fly on the wall when some corporate big wigs decided on that gem. Did anyone in the room suggest, "*Jack*, playing what you want"? Is it any wonder that satellite radio is kicking terrestrial radio's teeth down their throats? This slogan is a great lesson in how to lose a customer. For the record, while some *Jack* stations are doing okay, many are not.

Correcting other people's mistakes, even as a mental exercise, is an excellent way to keep up your sales chops. I'll bet you saw several ways to either fix *Jack's* problem or to effectively compete against them in the marketplace. (An interesting side note: Some of *Jack's* chief competitors started promoting formats that used the slogan "Playing What You Want." In many markets, they are outperforming *Jack*. What a surprise!)

One of my most embarrassing failures occurred when I was living in Atlanta. A magic bar had just opened, and as an amateur magician I decided it would be fun to perform there occasionally. Sleight-of-hand has been a hobby of mine for years. I auditioned and was accepted as a strolling close-up magician. It was a blast!

You're probably not surprised that I take a really different approach to magic. Sure, I love the effects, but I really love to entertain and make people laugh. My comedic and irreverent approach to close-up magic was a hit at this club. Because I was the creative director of a busy ad agency, I only took a few gigs a week so it wouldn't interfere with my day job. Eventually, I was getting so much laughter and applause the manager asked me to do the big weekend stage show. I was thrilled.

I practiced diligently for two weeks and I was ready. Forget the fact that I had been doing close-up, intimate magic for years before I ever performed in public. These two weeks of "intense practice" made me ready for the big stage...yeah, I can be pretty dense sometimes. Had I been an Eternal Student and examined what had worked for me in the past, I would have avoided a great deal of embarrassment (yes, modeling goes hand-in-hand with this discipline).

When the big night finally arrived, everything that could go wrong went wrong. I was awful. Things that were supposed to float fell to the floor. Things that were supposed to stay on the floor fell over.

It was one of the most embarrassing 90 minutes (it seemed like three weeks) of my life. "What do you mean that's not your card!"

So what's the bottom line? I was so bad that the owner never even asked me back to do close-up magic. I probably could have called him and sold myself, but I was just too embarrassed. Talk about continuing your education, it was a lesson I never forgot. It's okay to want to grow and be more, just don't make your move until you're more than ready. If you're a great close-up magician, mid-level manager or whatever, be proud of your accomplishments along with who and what you are. Make your move when the time is right for you.

A better course for me would have been to decline the big stage gig and really concentrate on the close-up magic that made me popular in the first place. The grass may be greener on the other side, but this side might be perfect for you or me.

Speaking of learning about sales from unconventional sources, I have gleaned a great deal of useful sales information from many non-sales books. The concept of "astonishment," as taught by magician and author Paul Harris in his *Art of Astonishment* trilogy (A-1 Multimedia, ©1996), has been particularly useful to me.

Paul states that the exact moment when the actual "magic" of any illusion occurs is one of the purest moments in the world of media. You can use this knowledge for your sales presentations and demonstrations. Here is an example.

I was demonstrating a big screen TV on Shop At Home. A few minutes into the presentation, without saying a word, I simply turned the TV sideways. Given its superior performance and image quality, the audience probably assumed that the TV was very thick and heavy.

After about two seconds of silence, I looked directly at the camera and said "This is how thin your new TV is." I then fell silent again for a moment and picked up the TV, saying, "And this is how light your new TV is."

Immediately after this, I went into a summary of the TV's most important benefits. I capitalized on the receptiveness of the audience after their moment of astonishment when their minds were open to new concepts. The presentation was tremendously successful.

Think about your product. What are some "astonishing" demonstrations you can do to capitalize on that "ah-ha" moment of astonishment? Formulate them, practice until they are second nature, and then effectively use a benefits-oriented close immediately thereafter. The results will be nothing short of *astonishing*.

I have read many reports about sales and motivational authors who achieved phenomenal success after self-publishing a book. In many cases, they created so much buzz on their own that a major publisher picked up their book. Others had so much success on their own that they made their mark without the help of a major publisher. Of course, there were those who refused to be an Eternal Student and failed miserably.

I think you'll agree (at least I hope you do) that this is a really different type of sales and motivational book. Taking a lead from many successful authors in this genre, I am publishing and promoting it myself. As someone who loves to teach and laugh, I hope this book helps a lot of people improve their sales techniques, whether they're selling a product or selling themselves. I'm marketing the book myself, modeling the success and techniques of many successful people. I'm always learning and then utilizing new ways to promote and advertise my book.

One of the most accurate measures of how dedicated you are to your craft as a salesperson is your level of commitment to constant improvement. The Japanese have a word for it: *Kaizen*. Sadly, there is no English equivalent. Those of us who are committed to getting better each and every day don't really need a word. We're satisfied in the success that comes with being an Eternal Student.

Infomercials: The Good, the Bad and the Extremely Ugly

You can learn a great deal about selling by studying infomercials. Long before I hosted them, I spent a great deal of time analyzing what worked and what didn't in this medium. The lessons I learned have helped me tremendously in all my sales efforts through the years. It also led me to quite a lucrative career.

I've done quite well in the infomercial world. I'm the host of the current Ron Popeil rotisserie and cutlery infomercials. I'm proud to say they are two of the highest grossing infomercials in the history of the medium. As a salesperson, you may be offered (or seek out) an opportunity to host and/or create a half hour infomercial or shorter direct response spot. In the industry, these are referred to as "long form and short form" spots.

Before you decide to look into this field, it might help to understand the background of this "cash cow" phenomenon.

We all know Ron Popeil created the first infomercial, right? Contrary to popular belief, the gifted inventor (he really is) was a virtual Johnny-Come-Lately in the field of electronic direct response marketing. The first true broadcast infomercial was a Chicago radio broadcast in 1927 by Reverend Paul Rader. The preacher figured that if he broadcast his church services on a local radio station, he could reach an entirely new congregation, passing them an electronic collection plate.

The gamble paid off, big time. The reverend's mail-in collections far exceeded the cost to air the broadcast. In 1928, taking his cue from this success, Reverend Donald Barnhouse bought time for his church on the fledgling CBS radio network. (This could explain a great deal about current Infinity programming). Again, his church prospered, taking in far more in collections than the cost of the airtime.

An industry was born, sort of. A church could solicit for donations without having to send anything in return. Prevailing limitations of the times made shipping products to individual homes difficult, if not impossible.

In those early days, most radio advertising consisted of conventional commercials urging consumers to buy a specific product or brand or shop at a particular store. This type of advertising remained in place for several decades.

In the 1950's, manufacturing and delivery technologies had advanced enough to allow direct response advertising, selling products directly to TV viewers and radio listeners. The amount of advertising time was not regulated. Anyone with enough money could buy a half hour on television (mostly live, video tape hadn't been invented) or radio and sell a product directly to the consumer.

Most of the early "pitchmen" came from county fairs, boardwalks, and in-store demonstrations. I remember when my mother came home from a seashore trip in the 1950's with a set of knives that had amazed her. I remember her saying, "They cut a tin can in half and then sliced a tomato so thin you could read a newspaper through it.," I've since discovered that virtually any serrated knife of any quality can do the same thing. It's not cutting, it's sawing.

Ron Popeil was one of the first people from this type of background to realize the power of television as a direct sales medium. As an amateur inventor at the time, he also knew that if you created the product you were selling, the profit potential was far greater than buying an existing product and reselling it.

Popeil spawned many imitators on both TV and radio, so many, in fact, that the government imposed new regulations limiting the amount of advertising time in each broadcast hour. This effectively ended the info-mercial industry at the time. Short form direct response ads (two minutes or less) remained, but with a few exceptions their effectiveness and profitability represented a small fraction of the success achieved by the half-hour spots.

As you will read elsewhere in this book, music was a big seller in the early days of television. On NBC, the recordings of the fabled NBC Orchestra were sold during and after on-air concerts. As you might think, these ads were very staid, conservative, and by today's standards, extremely boring. However, they did sell a lot of recordings. Although these early direct response ads were extremely laid back, they capitalized on the excitement of the moment, relying on the impulse response of the consumer. Remember, there were no 800 numbers (invented in the late 70's) or credit cards. You sent "cash, check or money order to Box XYZ, Grand Central Station, New York, New York."

Specialty music, such as polka, big band instrumental, and Christmas music, was also sold directly in the early days of TV. During the 1950's, regional polka bands, various novelty instrumental groups (The Harmonica Rascals and many of the Philadelphia String Bands were among the most popular), and various big bands (especially Benny Goodman and the Dorsey Brothers) sold large quantities of records on television. In most cases, these records were sold during regularly scheduled programs featuring the various artists. In the case of the Philadelphia String bands, the direct response spots ran during their appearance in the New Year's parade as well as in combination with commercials for their post-New Year series of concerts.

Except for music and few other gimmicky products, direct response advertising disappeared from radio as well. However, border radio stations (on the Mexico/ US border) used their half-million watt flamethrower signals to sell all manner of questionable products to the American Public. They sell everything from discount salvation to miracle electronic pain-relieving "thing-a-ma-bobs." Some stations offer their "advertisers" a complete package including Canadian P.O. boxes and offshore accounts to avoid any US interference.

It wasn't until 1984, when President Reagan deregulated television and radio, eliminating restrictions on the amount of commercial time within each hour, that long form infomercials were allowed back on the air. The floodgates were open. Within a few years, thousands of infomercials were produced for TV and radio. Stations anxious to increase their billing especially in the historically dead overnight periods, accepted any and all half-hour infomercials.

Unfortunately for the consumer, there were few government regulations that dealt with the quality of the products and the validity of the claims that were made. Infomercial products could cure cancer, give you more energy (which is now illegal to claim for any ingestible product) or make you a millionaire overnight.

Enter the Federal Trade Commission and the Food and Drug Administration. It didn't take long for the complaints to come in by the thousands. People still had cancer, no energy, and now that they had shelled out their hard-earned dollars for useless products, many of them were broke. The FTC and FDA began hearing cases and creating regulations. Sadly, the wheels of government turn slowly and many useless products made their sellers rich before they were stopped.

Not to say that all TV and radio infomercial products are worthless. Some reputable infomercial producers like California's Guthy Renker would only sell a product if it met their very strict guidelines, often more stringent than government regulations.

The origin of the Home Shopping Network, the first major televised shopping channel, predates the 1984 commercial time deregulation. In 1977, a Florida radio station accepted 112 electric can openers as payment for a delinquent account. They sold the can openers on-air, selling them all in a few minutes. The station began selling more and more products directly to their listeners. In the early 1980's, they bought time on a local cable station for the sole purpose of selling products.

These multi-hour televised "bargathons" were perfectly legal from a broadcast standpoint, since they were on cable, which was not heavily regulated by the government. However, in order to increase sales, their hosts began to make exaggerated claims about everything from the efficacy of the products to the actual monetary savings, attracting further government attention. In the late 1980's, government agencies began to impose strict regulations on the infomercial industry especially regarding television broadcasts.

As a result of this, radio infomercials began to increase in popularity. They cost less to produce and air, making them very profitable, if the product was popular. It's interesting to note that only 1 in 20 infomercials (either on TV or radio) ever make money. But when they do, the money can be incredible. That's why you hear the same few infomercials running over and over on both TV and radio. They're the ones making big money.

As HSN and QVC (founded in 1987) made televised shopping a popular national pastime, radio infomercials were truly "under the radar." The FTC, FDA, and other regulatory agencies were too busy with the multi-billion televised shopping industry to pay much attention to radio. That's all it took.

Dozens, if not hundreds of totally ineffective ingestible products hit the radio airwaves. These companies even had "war chests" with millions of dollars put aside to cover the fines and legal bills they would have to pay as cost to do business. Some of these companies made millions, even after paying a hefty fine. They would simply pay their fine, pocket their money, go out of business and start all over again.

Not all companies selling ingestible products are scam artists. Some supplements sold on radio infomercials really do work as claimed. There are some reputable companies who make and sell good products at a fair price via radio infomercials. And their inventors and spokespeople make totally legitimate claims. Unfortunately, these people are the exception, not the rule.

On the "Dark Side," while claims made by the creators of health and fitness products and radio stations are strictly regulated, statements made by uncompensated consumers, are not, hence, the "Testimonial Call." People are joiners; they want to be on a winning team. If product X cured Ethel from Des Moines' gout, then it will cure mine. So what if Ethel is 21 healthy and fit, and I'm 82 and in very bad health.

Any listener/viewer testimonial must be taken with a large grain of salt, even if you're on a sodium-restricted diet. Someone taking the time to call in and extol the virtues of any product, especially an ingestible one, is trying to help. However, given all the variables of the human condition, these calls may do more harm than good.

HSN and QVC run frequent disclaimers stating something like, "You may hear viewers calling in to give their opinions of a particular product. The views they express represent only their opinions and not those of the network or any of its affiliates. But we really want your calls." I've yet to hear any such warnings on a radio infomercial. The bottom line is *Caveat Emptor*.

Because of the uncontrollable nature of these calls, before they are permitted to go on-air, the government now requires the live TV shopping channels to collect detailed data about the people making the claims. Pre-recorded radio and TV infomercials must also collect this data for their testimonial calls.

Let's not forget the old throwaway line "Your results may vary." Legally, it must now be stated, "Your results ***will*** vary." Still, most people who are watching or listening to an infomercial at 3 AM are looking for something and will hear only what they want to hear. Even the late Dr. James Corea, the king of the health and fitness infomercial in the Philadelphia market, used to say, "If there were a magic pill to lose weight without eating less or exercising, don't you think a major pharmaceutical company would own it and sell it for a thousand bucks a pop? And people would pay it."

It's interesting to note that several different "miracle" weight loss products marketed through TV and radio infomercials made millions of dollars, even after the FDA deemed them to be totally ineffective. Their makers went on to make so much money that they "happily" paid the millions of dollars in fines that were levied.

Infomercials have sometimes heralded the eventual demise of a radio station (or at least its current format). In the short term they do make money for the people selling the products and the stations who run them. Unchecked, they can literally ruin a station's format. Philadelphia lost its FM talker, WWDB, in large part because constant infomercials made it unlistenable.

If you get the opportunity to host an infomercial, there are a few important things to keep in mind. First and foremost, do your homework. You aren't supposed to be an expert, that's why you have a guest. Still, you need to know as much about the product as possible.

Also realize that this is broadcasting. Most infomercial hosts are actors, TV or radio hosts. I am fortunate to be both a salesperson as well as a TV and radio host, so the transition was relatively easy for me.

If you did some broadcasting in college, that's a good first step, but probably not enough. There are industry professionals in most major cities who offer relatively inexpensive courses that teach you how to act in commercials. Some colleges and universities offer these courses as well.

Take one of these before throwing your hat into the infomercial ring. I firmly believe that great sales skills are more important than your "media chops," when it comes to infomercials. Still, I owe my success in this arena to the fact that I have been trained in both disciplines. Remember the chapter on modeling?

Before you sign anything, ask to have your attorney speak with the company's attorney, questioning him or her extensively about the claims that can be legally made about the product. Also ask about your liability. As the host, are you liable for claims made by the product's representatives and customers? If so, you have some heavy decisions to make.

If the product is ingestible and they tell you that you are as responsible for product liability as the company – run! Never, ever host an infomercial if you are going to be held accountable for any product liability. Have it put in writing!

The company's attorney can write up a simple indemnification document that you both will have to sign. Unfortunately, even then, if there is any litigation or breach of law, you could still be dragged into court and the validity of your indemnification agreement might come into question.

Where is the upside for you? A lot of money for very little work, if you do it right. Before you sign anything, make sure you are getting a piece of the "back end," which is a percentage of the sales of the product, in addition to a performance fee. How much? It's difficult to say, but you should definitely hire a lawyer familiar with infomercials and/or direct response marketing to negotiate your contract. Check with your local bar association. It will be more than worth the expense.

Even if you have the right deal in place, keep in mind that fewer than 1 in 20 infomercials ever makes money. The success or failure is based on many factors, but in all cases, product is king. The best "pitch" will fall on deaf ears if the product isn't right. And even with the right product, the upsell products have to be right as well.

In many cases, the main product of the infomercial just pays for the airtime. Many companies have a business model that is dependent on how many "accessories" their telephone representatives can convince you to buy. Most infomercial companies are not concerned with how much this practice will annoy their customers. Their business model is built on the concept of the upsell.

If you have the right deal in place and the infomercial succeeds, you are in for a windfall. Imagine making money while you are sleeping. Mailbox money is a wonderful thing!

How does someone say, "Screw you!" in the world of direct response marketing? Let me count the ways. Since I had worked with him on QVC, guitarist Esteban asked me to host his first infomercial. It was my first infomercial as well. He said, "Hey, bro, you're my friend, I'm doing this on my own, I don't have a lot of money to spend, I can't afford your usual performance fee, I can't give you a percentage..." The list went on.

I didn't even know what my "usual performance fee" was; let alone how much I was losing by not getting a percentage of sales. I agreed to do the show for a few thousand dollars. Esteban went on to sell hundreds of thousands of guitars.

I know there's even a parable in the Bible about being happy with the deal you make. Okay, I'm happy that I lost tens of thousands of dollars. It was an expensive education, but it's a lesson I will never forget. Hey, he's a great guy, a marvelous guitarist and a much better businessperson than I at the time. If we do business in the future, I'll know what to ask for and how to get it.

I'm lucky that Ron Popeil is one of my closest friends. After seeing me in the Esteban spot, he asked me to host his latest rotisserie infomercial. I agreed, and he asked me how much I wanted. He's my friend and I have always had a problem doing business with my friends. I asked him to pay me what he considered to be fair. He did and I am delighted with the arrangement. I've done very well from both the Ronco infomercials I've hosted and we did it all on a handshake. That's the kind of guy Ron is. But unless the person asking you to host an infomercial is like a brother or sister to you, get a lawyer and get it in writing.

How will hosting an infomercial affect your credibility? After all, there is a stigma attached to the industry.

Unfortunately, it's a stigma that's been earned by too many unscrupulous companies. When someone I meet takes a cheap shot at one of the infomercials I've done, I just tell them it's a commercial, albeit a long one. I don't find it any different than the current crop of celebrities who host commercials for many different products and services.

To help maintain my credibility and keep me out of court, I also maintain a strict policy of never hosting any ingestible products, either on radio or television. Ingestibles offer the greatest opportunity for litigation. I realize that might seem pretty drastic, but I feel there are enough legal hassles in life without openly inviting more. Hopefully, the information in this chapter will help you make the right decision.

An interesting final note: I was recently offered the opportunity to host a "male enhancement" product infomercial. This herbal tablet not only added an extra three inches, where it counts, it "ensured" that the additional length would be extremely firm. They wanted me to use the product for a month and give a personal testimonial. I can see it now, "Hello, I'm Steve Bryant. I used to be impotent and have a small..."

Selling Music on Television

Like the chapter on infomercials, this obviously specialized subject matter contains some excellent examples of positioning, focus and many other sales strategies and techniques that you will find useful no matter what you are selling. And since we've all seen the direct response spots from Time-Life, K-Tel, Ronco and many others, you should find it pretty cool to "peek behind the curtain."

Introduction

Music is a temporal art. Unlike painting and sculpture, it needs time to exist. That presents various problems in a medium like television, where time is the most precious commodity. To better understand these inherent difficulties, let's take a brief look at some of the more interesting highlights of the history of music commerce on TV.

The Past

Selling music on television is as old as commercial television itself. As stated in the previous chapter, the recordings of the fabled NBC Orchestra were sold, quite successfully during and after on-air concerts in the 1950's.

As you also learned in the last chapter, specialty music, such as polka, big band instrumental, and Christmas music was also sold directly in the early days of TV. During the 1950's, regional polka bands, various novelty instrumental groups (The Harmonica Rascals and many of the Philadelphia String Bands, among the most popular), and various big bands (especially Benny Goodman and the Dorsey Brothers) sold enormous numbers of records on television

Ads for compilation records (Greatest Hits collections) began to run in the late 50's. The infamous K-Tel and Ronco companies were at the forefront of this movement. Both companies (who later merged into one mega-company) bought the master recordings for various Greatest Hits collections, negotiated substantially lower (sometimes nonexistent) royalty rates for the artists and publishers, and released attractively priced record collections. These were sold using 60 and 120-second direct response television spots. Keep in mind, these early-televised music sales happened in the days before toll-free numbers and the proliferation of credit cards. The ads urged viewers to send "cash, check or money order" to the company's mailing address, which was repeated so many times that even the most forgetful viewer could recite it in his or her sleep. They sold millions per year.

Media-created "Superstars" began to surface in the 1960's and 70's, modeling their campaigns after the novelty acts of the 1950's. Utilizing all the tools of the direct response advertiser, these ads created musical careers out of thin air. Millions of Boxcar Willie, Slim Whitman, Zamfir and Roger Whittaker albums were sold. Viewers were eager to hear the music of artists who "outsold the Beatles" in a few small, little-known countries.

It's interesting to note that when the major record labels tried to release the music from most of these artists through standard retail channels, they failed miserably.

The one exception was Zamfir, whose 1980's success was a direct result of the use of his music in the successful *Karate Kid* movies.

Most of the direct response TV ads ran right after the Christmas, capitalizing on the fact that many people received cash gifts. Even Christmas music sold well in the first few weeks after Christmas.

The 70's saw the birth of direct response music giants like Heartland Music and Time-Life Music. They were among the first companies to realize the importance of continuity programs, like "Greatest Hits of the 50's," where you would receive one record every 6-to-8 weeks for an extended time. The complete collection might comprise a dozen or more records and end up costing hundreds of dollars, but the consumer was only required to pay for one record at a time. It was a brilliant move that was successfully modeled by many companies. With today's payment plan options, the record companies send their customers the entire collection, allowing them to pay for it over a course of months.

The profit margin was large enough in these huge

collections to allow the production and airing of half-hour infomercials. A "celebrity" host (usually a famous DJ, television, or music personality) would narrate the history of whatever era was being sold. These programs were fun to watch and gave the viewer a great deal of trivia and behind-the-scenes information. Most were (and many still are) extremely successful.

By contrast, shopping channels have had spotty sucess selling music over the years. By comparing what has worked on television in the past and the musical sales endeavors of these cable-shopping channels, it's easy to identify what works in televised musical merchandising now and what will work in the future.

A Temporal Art

If you look at the common threads of the successful short and long form direct response TV ads selling music, one main fact stands out. The more music that was played, the more music was sold. It is as simple as that. Spots that droned on and on with extended discussion and narration failed. Additionally, there is a correlation between how many times the ads stated how much music the customer received (number of songs and/or play time) and the success of the ad. As a temporal art, much of the value of music is inherent in how much listening time you receive.

In an age when people watch TV with their thumbs poised firmly on the remote control, this temporal aspect is more important than ever. While you can stress it so much that it becomes annoying, it would be better to err on the side of too much rather than too little. Remember, viewers are constantly tuning in and out.

Music versus Artist

In the history of selling music on television, how important is the artist? In the big picture, he or she is not all that important. On QVC, the earliest John Tesh presentations stressed his background, musical education, TV credentials, etc. All of these presentations failed. On the same weekend day, Tesh sold 2300 copies of a three-CD package at 1 p.m. and 13,000 at 4 p.m. The host for the 1 p.m. presentation interviewed Tesh extensively about his background, allowing the artist to play 1½ songs (they faded out the last one). The 4 p.m. host told the viewers how many songs they received, how much time the collection "occupied," and talked very little to the artist, allowing him to play four songs in the same time period. Three guesses who that host was?

People who are buying music are buying entertainment. If they like what they hear and are convinced that they are getting enough entertainment for their money, they are very likely to buy.

The success of Giovanni, like Tesh, a pianist/composer, on QVC and HSN is another interesting case to study. Much like Boxcar Willie and Slim Whitman, this artist had no history in this country. He did play a pleasant type of instrumental music and used the medium of television with the skill of a 90's Ozzie Nelson. Utilizing superimposed videotaped images and striking a prayer-like pose after playing, this artist pandered to the spiritual nature of his 40+ female audience.

Giovanni rarely played live, choosing to "finger-sync" his performances. This led to many obviously prerecorded fadeouts. It didn't matter to his audience. They were getting hours of music for a few dollars from a man whose music "came from God." It was marketing brilliance.

Giovanni's sales began to slump when hosts started questioning him about his background so much they left little time for him to "play." They also didn't stress the amount of music (number of songs and running time) in his collection. Many Giovanni performances turned into talk fests between the host, the artist, and the viewers who called in. All of these appearances failed.

The most successful Giovanni presentation was a full hour show where he played 14 songs in one hour, talking briefly to members of the live audience about his music, not his background, his *music*. During Giovanni's performance breaks, the host modeled the long form music infomercials by issuing a subtle call to action between each song. That call to action consisted of identifying the value, i.e., the number of songs and playtime, suggesting that the viewer call in now so he or she wouldn't miss the next song.

Of course, an artist must be positioned (credentials and background), but that can be done in a sentence or two. Any more than that will begin to impact playing and selling time.

In his most successful hour, Giovanni sold over 30,000 CDs, which got the attention of Atlantic records who signed the artist and released an "As Seen on TV" package of his original material. This recording did not succeed. Why? Read on.

Is It a Toe Tapper?

Giovanni's success was due in large part to the selection of his music. Most were familiar tunes that people could hum or sing. He included a few originals on each CD (artists make more money this way), but most of his selections were instrumental versions of popular songs. Along with value, the television customer wants familiar music. Direct response spots for "forgotten classics" (and there have been quite a few) have all failed. If the public forgot it, it probably wasn't worth redoing.

Giovanni's Atlantic CD contained mostly original songs. Without the hype of TV and background videos, he was just another "New Age" artist, most of whom sell fewer than 5000 recordings a year. By having only a few recognizable tunes on this collection, Giovanni assured his conventional (bricks and mortar) retail failure.

In addition to featuring familiar tunes, most successful TV music campaigns feature instrumental music. Obviously, Greatest Hits collections are a major exception to this rule. While there are a few other exceptions (most notably Roger Whittaker, The Three Tenors, and Slim Whitman), the majority of successful TV campaigns were for instrumental music. Most industry data seems to indicate that people perceive instrumental music as "universal music." It's music that you can listen to all the time: while working, having conversations, driving, falling asleep. There are no vocals to compete with whatever you are doing

History has proven that vocal music must be exceptional, truly extraordinary and *different* to be successful. The voices of three of the most successful direct response TV artists, Roger Whittaker, The Three Tenors and even Slim Whitman (not too many yodeling, nasal singing cowboys on the market these days) meet these criteria. Even some of music's top crooners have tried and failed to sell their music on television. Good and *different* is the key.

I hope you see how this applies to you as a salesperson, regardless of what you sell. What's different about your company and product? How do those differences benefit your customer? In which ways do the differences set you apart from your competition?

Look around at successful companies and products. Are they the "same old, same old" products or are they really different from the competition? In most cases, you will find successful products to be quite unique.

What can you do to effectively communicate the differences (and inherent benefits) of your products to your customers? If the late (and actually quite talented) Boxcar Willie can sell millions of records because he offered his customers something different than the mainstream music community, your products' differences, widely known as *Unique Selling Propositions*, could help to make your company and you quite wealthy.

The Televised Rise and Fall of Robert Bonfiglio

The success of harmonica virtuoso Robert Bonfiglio on QVC is an interesting study in what sells music, and what doesn't. Bonfiglio was a very well known concert and blues harmonica player in serious musical circles. Because of the public perception of the harmonica (or lack thereof) he was never a popular artist with the masses. Even a major release on RCA didn't gain him major public acceptance.

During his first appearance on QVC, he played almost four abbreviated songs (allowing time for calls to action) during a 14-minute spot. His music sold out. He began producing material exclusively for QVC. Most CD and tape sets sold out. His appearances on QVC put him on the national charts as one of the best selling new age instrumentalist of the mid-90's. He even out-sold John Tesh, who was one of the hottest new age artists at that time.

He did a two-CD/tape Christmas collection that sold almost 10,000 copies in a 12-minute airing and thousands more in additional airings. Again, the presentations were about the music; the artist was secondary. In all the presentations, the customer was constantly reminded of what he or she received. The number of songs included and the amount of play time were both stressed throughout the presentations. Additionally, the fact that the music was played on the harmonica was emphasized.

The incredible tone Bonfiglio was able to produce on the "lowly" harmonica made the music truly different. That difference helped to define it and sell it.

Then, everything went wrong. There is an old saying, "Bulls make money, bears make money and hogs get slaughtered." Since Bonfiglio had a best selling Christmas collection, it was decided to do another. And this one would have vocals, lots of vocals. The guiding force behind this change in direction decided that in order to have a radio "hit," Bonfiglio needed a song with vocals (with the way he was selling, who needed radio?). Although many people at QVC raised cautionary flags about the lack of focus in the new collection, the project was approved. It was even decided that Bonfiglio would do a PBS special based on the CD. Although Robert is a very educated man, he was completely out of his element hosting the show. It looked amateurish at best.

The CD was a debacle as well. Combined with the fact that every really good Christmas song had been covered in his previous release, the lack of focus doomed the project. Sales for the CD set were extremely low and the project was dropped.

He has not been back on direct response television since. Hopefully, he will return. His talent is enormous and his instrumental music is truly enjoyable. I'm willing to bet that any new project will focus on Bonfiglio's instrumental genius. Focus sells, there's no doubt about it!

Overall, history has proven that selling unfocused music (combinations of instrumental and vocal music of the same type) is tricky at best. Aside from Greatest Hits and holiday collections, no set of vocal and instrumental music has fared well on direct response television. And, although Greatest Hits and holiday collections usually contain a combination of vocal and instrumental music (a majority of which is vocal music), their focus is derived from their genre. To generate sales, both rely on the memories evoked by the music rather than the individual songs.

The best sales results for unfocused music resulted from focusing on one element of a collection. Obviously, if it's primarily vocal, concentrate on those songs, or vise versa. Many times, although there is not a holiday or Greatest Hits focus, one can be created by using a phase like, "Thirty-four of your instrumental favorites, along with some of the most popular vocal music of all time." Another effective phrase is, "Over two hours of your vocal favorites as well as many best-selling instrumental hits." In both phrases, the temporal nature (amount of music) is highlighted while the positive aspects of the package are clearly focused. In many cases, the sheer number of songs or play time can be used as a focus for a particular collection.

How is your focus as a salesperson? Are your presentations and proposals focused on the exact products that your customers need? Or, are they scattered, giving your customer too many choices? The incredible focus of successful music campaigns on television has been a template for some of my most successful sales presentations. These televised music sales campaigns have really taught me to focus my sales presentations and continually substantiate the value of the offer to my customer.

And the Hits Just Keep on Coming.

Greatest Hits and holiday collections are truly collections of memories. If a song evokes a strong memory, the viewer will want to relive that memory, doing so every time that song is played.

The same rule of thumb applies to Greatest Hits collections. Memories create sales. All the successful short form direct response ads weave memories into their presentations by asking the viewer questions beginning with the phrases:

"Who were you with...?"
"What were you doing...?"
"Where were you...?"
"When did you...?"
"Why did those times...?"
"How much fun...?"
"Do you remember...?"

Notice that the first five questions use the standard criteria for lead paragraphs of good newspaper copy, "who, what, where, when, and why." They are also excellent methods for creating questions designed to stimulate pleasant memories. Keep in mind that all successful presentations are about the music. In a live direct response situation, it's best to ask one question of an artist or guest, issue a call to action to the audience, and then play lots of music.

Graphic scrolls of all the music in the collection should be used while playing the music. If there is a book accompanying the collection, it should be thumbed through on camera while the music is playing and the scroll is running. If this seems like sensory over-load, it is. Think of sports bars, where there is live or recorded music playing, several TVs tuned to different sporting events, video games, crowd noise and more.

By the way, questions are great closers that can be used almost anytime in a sales presentation. If you watch any successful music infomercial, or other direct response presentation, you will notice that many times the questions asked by the host are excellent-yet-subtle calls to action. For example, a question like, "What does this collection mean to you?" can trigger a sales response if the answer is right. You don't think they leave that to chance, do you? The answer has been carefully written and rehearsed.

Do you wait until the end of the sales presentation to close? Hopefully not. You should be closing from the moment you begin your presentation. I can't tell you how many times a customer has bought from me well before I finished my sales pitch...and I don't think they were trying to get rid of me. I substantiated the value of my product and asked questions that would give me the information I needed to close the sale.

All the research I've done concerning effective ways to sell music on television has helped me come up with new and innovative ideas for all types of sales presentations. As I stated earlier in this book, you can learn a great deal about sales from studying what has worked in many different disciplines.

A Guest Fest

Many times, holiday and Greatest Hits collections come with an "expert" guest. While oftentimes this guest creates credibility and excitement that adds to sales, the presentation is still about the music. The guest should be instructed to speak in "sound bites," and as much music as possible should be played. It has also been proven to be very effective to play music in the background during the entire presentation. It's another way to ensure that the presentation is "about the music."

If you use experts to add credibility to your sales presentations, use them carefully. Make sure they know to speak succinctly and stress the benefits of your products, not just their intricate workings. Just like music sales are about the music much more than the artist, your sales presentations should be focused on the benefits your product provides to your customer. A properly coached expert can be a great help. An unrehearsed expert brought along to simply make a good impression could be nightmare.

Heroes and Villains

There are some artists whose popularity is so great that their success on direct response television is almost guaranteed. On QVC, this has included artists such as Alabama, Barry Manilow and Kenny G. Even though the Beatles broke up almost 30 years ago and Elvis has been dead for over a quarter of a century, they both enjoy great success on QVC and other televised outlets. But it's interesting to note that music sales for all these artists are great for the first few airings then they drop off dramatically. The most plausible explanation for this phenomenon is that once the core fans have made their purchases, they are waiting for more new music.

Again, it's about the music. By using the techniques described in this chapter, sales for these superstars could be increased. Emphasizing the music, its temporal nature, relating the value, exclusivity, etc. are all factors that have proven time and time again to increase music sales. Utilizing these techniques could greatly increase the longevity of the direct response success enjoyed by even the most popular artists.

Think about your sales presentations, which I hope you do quite often. Are they completely focused on the benefits your customers will derive from using your products? Or do you waste time elaborating on nuts and bolts, rather than features and benefits. More than likely, your customer knows what your product is. He or she wants to know what it can do for them.

Busted Flat on QVC

Kris Kristofferson's initial lack of success on QVC is an interesting study. One of the best selling songwriters of all time, Kristofferson's *The Austin Sessions* CD did not sell that well during his first presentation.

For his first airing, QVC had the exclusive debut of *The Austin Sessions*. The exclusivity factor alone is a powerful sales motivator. Add to that the fact that Austin is a major singer songwriter capital of the country and that this was the second in the Austin series (Jimmy Webb's CD was the first), and you have a lot of reasons to own this collection. It contained all of Kristofferson's greatest hits. Although they were re-recorded (usually the kiss-of-death in musical circles), they were recorded using state-of-the-art technology in a city synonymous with musical greatness. Add the fact that most of the songs had sold millions when recorded by other artists and you have a very powerful sales story.

Unfortunately, the first host who interviewed Kristofferson centered on the man, not his music. The questions were lengthy, and the host didn't even know the name of his greatest hit ("Me and Bobby Magee" was referred to as "Busted Flat in Baton Rouge"). The artist did correct the host; however, the lack of focus (the audience was never told why *The Austin Sessions* was special) and the lengthy questions and discussion allowed little time for Kristofferson's band to play music. The first presentation failed.

I'm pleased to say that his second presentation was a rousing success. This time I was the host and made sure I understood why this collection was important. I also issued strong calls to action between every song. Most importantly, while I was extremely respectful to Kris Kristofferson, I made sure that the presentation focused on the music. I let the customer know how much they received and why it was important. The CD sold very well, both the artist and the network were very happy.

An on-air host for a musical act does not need to be a musicologist to know the facts about Kris Kristofferson noted in this chapter. Most pertinent facts are covered in the artist's press release. Larry King openly admits he doesn't read the books or listen to the CDs from his guests, yet he asks great questions. If he doesn't read the artist's press release, the person "feeding" him the information through his earpiece certainly does.

In a televised sales situation, questions must be brief and phrased so that the answer is also concise. Again, one question that has always worked well during a televised presentation is, "What makes this CD (or song) special to you?" Remember, the key is "less talk and more music."

The success of the musical group Trains-Siberian Orchestra on QVC is a perfect example of a well-done musical presentation. The group plays a really different type of Christmas music. As mentioned earlier in this chapter, the difference of the music helps to define it. During the QVC spot, the artist was interviewed minimally, allowing for three songs to be played during the 12-minute presentation.

Mannheim Steamroller is another example of distinctive Christmas music. Founder Chip Davis and his entourage have done extraordinarily well selling their music on QVC and elsewhere. In fact, Mannheim Steamroller's story is a great sales lesson. Chip Davis decided that he was going to re-invent Christmas music. He did just that, and if you've ever heard Mannheim Steamroller, you know how different and truly marvelous their music is.

He also understands the sales process better than any other musician I've ever met (he's not only the founder but also the drummer and arranger for Mannheim

Steamroller). Every year, he appeared on QVC in October to sell his music. In the world of Christmas music, most people add only one new CD to their collection every year. He was always the first artist to sell Christmas music on the network, and it paid off. Each year he outsold any other Christmas artist. He was even written up in Billboard Magazine (one of the most important periodicals in the music industry) for his televised success.

In the world of sales, regardless of what you're selling, you can rarely be too early, even for Christmas music.

The Art of the Guitar

Unknown artists can be more successful selling their music on television than established performers. One interesting case in point is Esteban, mentioned in the previous chapter. Esteban is a fine guitarist, composer and performer. He has overcome many tragedies, including an accident that left him visually impaired and unable to play for more than a decade.

Esteban impressed guitar virtuoso Segovia so much that he became one of his prized pupils. Segovia even gave the young guitarist his stage name "Esteban."

Unfortunately, like so many talented artists, Esteban struggled for many years, performing at various venues and selling self-produced CDs to earn a living. His talent wasn't enough to ensure his success until one day a very intuitive entrepreneur happened to hear him playing at a resort and brought him to QVC.

The cable shopping giant was wary of airing an unknown artist to its millions of viewers. The entrepreneur and Esteban arranged to give a free concert for QVC employees. This non-broadcast event created a huge buzz in the building.

Sometimes a free sample can make all the difference in a sales situation. If you haven't tried it, you're missing out on a great sales tool.

Because of the great word-of-mouth that resulted from Esteban's free concert, he was invited to sell his music on-air, but was given a 1 a.m. time, not usually considered a prime slot.

As the host for the presentation, I spent several hours speaking with Esteban and the entrepreneur prior to the presentation. Each collection of music was categorized and differentiated.

One collection was the "Romantic Collection," another was "Latin," yet an- other was dubbed "Relaxing." This focus defined each collection and gave the audience a reason to purchase each set.

Questions were formulated to keep answers to a minimum, allowing for more music to be played. The exclusivity of the music was stressed in the presentation, "Available only on QVC or at Esteban performances."

The hour set an all time record for the 1 a.m. slot on QVC, grossing over $200,000. A subsequent prime time hour grossed over $350,000, setting a record for televised music sales that stood for years. Again, the "less talk, more music" format was utilized. The number of songs and running time of each set was also stressed throughout the presentations.

The entrepreneur who brought Esteban to QVC was lured away by QVC's main competitor, the Home Shopping Network, taking Esteban to the Florida-based televised shopping channel. HSN used its industry contacts to procure a major recording contract for Esteban. This double-barreled approach of in-store sales combined with on-air appearances on HSN proved to be successful, although never to the initial levels of Esteban's QVC appearances.

I believe one primary reason for Esteban's lower televised CD sales is HSN's insistence of having one of its hosts on the set while he is performing. This type of "bench warmer," usually a female who "swoons" as Esteban plays detracts from the focus of the artist and his music. This allows the audience to be distracted, making them less likely to buy. One can only assume that the "swooner" is present because of the "that's the way we've always done it" mentality present in many major corporations today.

A new recording takes a great deal of time to produce and release. Regardless of any initial success, CD sales quickly decline in the closed environment of a televised shopping network. Given the customer's voracious appetite for new products, Esteban switched his focus from selling CD's to selling guitars and how-to videos. He has been tremendously successful at this. He still sells his CD's on HSN, but now takes the time necessary to produce quality new material.

Just like Esteban, if your product line is getting a bit stale, find some related products to add to your line. Not to the point of brand extension, which rarely works, but good solid complementary products that could round out your line. It might sound simplistic, but you'd be surprised how many companies struggle because they refuse to tamper with the status quo. I knew there was a reason I wrote the "But That's the Way We've Always Done It" chapter.

The Future of Music Sales

Downloadable music (primarily MP3) from the Internet is changing the nature of selling music on television and everywhere else. The Internet is having a phenomenal impact on music sales, both at conventional retail and on TV. To continue to be a major factor in the sales of music, direct response television will have to keep pace with these new technologies. A televised sales presentation could instruct viewer to go to a website for some free downloads, allowing them to sample the music before buying. They could then order the entire collection on CD or pay to download it immediately. Thanks to the Internet, the possibilities are endless.

Summary -- Techniques for Selling Music on Television

1. Music sales are about the music! The more music that's played, the more music that's sold.
2. Reread technique #1.
3. Music is a temporal art. People are buying an amount of music. The more they understand about how much they are getting for their money, the more likely they are to buy.
4. While the artist is important, he or she is never as important as the music.
5. The selection of music is an integral part of the success of music on television. The better-known the music is, the better it sells.
6. Historically, instrumental music has sold better than vocal music on television.
7. If the music being sold is different in one or more ways than other types of similar music, the difference defines it, focuses it and sets it apart from the competition.
8. Focus is a major key in the success of music on television. An all-instrumental or all vocal package is more focused than a package that mixes the two.

9. Memories are the most effective focus to use when selling Greatest Hits and Holiday collections.
10. If possible, ask an artist about his or her work prior to the presentation. At very least, read the press release thoroughly. With more information, you'll be able to minimize your interview, allowing more music to be played.

I hope you gleaned some concepts and techniques for your own sales presentations from this chapter. Great ideas can come from almost anywhere. In the world of sales, take the time to study what has worked in a completely different field than your own. You'll be amazed at how much you'll learn as your sales continue to increase. Good selling!

Winners and Losers

The examples in this chapter actually fit in several different chapters, so I didn't know exactly where to put them. Since they contain some very valuable selling ideas and techniques, I thought I'd create a special multi-disciplinary chapter for them. The first example is one of the saddest stories I know, probably because it's about one of my biggest losses. I call it:

It Seemed Like a Good Idea at the Time

I retired from QVC after 15 years and did some professional things I always wanted to do, including music, talk radio, and hosting some infomercials. After three years on my own, I received a call from an old QVC friend who told me she was now at Shop At Home in Nashville, the nation's 4th largest televised shopping channel. Even though they had been in business for 16 years, she noted that it reminded her of the first few years at QVC. Since those had been my favorite times at QVC and she said they were looking for an executive to guide them to the next level, I went down for an interview.

Instead of an interview, they made me do an on-camera audition. I had racked up over 15,000 hours of live TV time at QVC and was responsible for some of the biggest successes in the company's history. And these guys were insisting on an audition? Okay, I took my slightly bruised ego and did an audition. After this, the company's president told me that they might be interested in using me on-air, with a few additional responsibilities. I thanked her and told her if I had wanted to stay on-air I would have remained at QVC. I flew home, fairly certain I wouldn't hear from her again.

A few weeks later, she called and offered me a Vice Presidential position with about ten hours of on-air hosting each week. Confident in the fact that I could dazzle them with my understanding of the industry and get off the air pretty quickly, I was on my way to Nashville.

My first day there, the president came into my office and told me that my first month would be spent doing nothing but watching Shop At Home, so I would understand what they did. Despite the fact that I told her I was an absolute geek about all shopping channels and was recognized as one of the leading experts in the field, she let me know there would be trouble if I didn't comply with her wishes.

If I hadn't already bought a house in town, I would have been headed back to Pennsylvania that day. However, I got to know her schedule and was always in my office dutifully watching the channel every time she walked by. Other times, away from prying eyes, I was coaching and training the sales staff and making some great progress. Now I know how Clint Eastwood felt in *Escape from Alcatraz*.

A few months later, I was sitting with a couple of people from merchandising trying to strategize the sale of a big screen TV. We had made an excellent buy and were going to be able to offer the customers a terrific value. Modeling some techniques from QVC, I suggested trying to sell the entire quantity in a single day. This would result in the largest day in company history.

Again modeling what had worked in the past, I created a strategy that included a special on-air promo that told our customers we had a great value for them, so special that we couldn't tell them until its debut. I also coached the hosts, giving them new and innovative techniques to use for the on-air sales presentations.

It worked! We had the biggest day in company history, selling all of the TVs in one day. We were heroes, right? I wish I could say yes, but, along with my two colleagues from merchandising, I was handed my head. It seems that we didn't include the president's handpicked people when we created the strategy. The president was livid, telling us that if we ever did that again, there would be serious consequences.

Instead of trying to sell her on the benefits of allowing us to continue to do this type of promotion, I took the offensive, arguing instead of selling. Hindsight being 20/20, I know I could have convinced her to allow us to continue if I had used my sales skills, instead of engaging her in useless debates. Of course, telling her that in my opinion her people were "idiots" didn't help either. Hey, when I blow it, I really blow it.

We tried to include her people, but they just didn't get what we were trying to do. But again, I argued my points during meetings instead of trying to sell them.

Almost every meeting became an adversarial gathering. It was very frustrating.

We kept losing money at an alarming rate. By the time we got a new president who happened to be a skilled merchant, it was too late. In June of 2006, Shop At Home was sold by Scripps to the Jewelry Network. They continue now with a greatly reduced staff and completely different focus.

If you are ever in a similar situation, don't argue, sell your heart out. I guarantee that from now on, I will!

Radio Gets Sirius (and XM)

I've learned a lot from my lifelong association with radio, but never more than I've learned by studying the advent and ongoing success of satellite radio. It's a lesson in sales brilliance and ultimate customer service

For decades, terrestrial radio was a primary source for information and entertainment. Even with the arrival of television, radio flourished from the 1950's right through the early 1990's. After a series of governmental deregulatory moves, large corporations moved in and began to consolidate their operations.

This quickly resulted in a loss of local programming and literally gutted any personality out of the medium.

Radio has become as bland and uninteresting as the mega corporations who now own it. As more and more people turn to CDs and iPods for their driving entertainment, listenership keeps dropping. A few talk stations are flourishing by pandering to a growing right wing audience. But music radio is dying.

The innovators of XM and Sirius radio are mostly disenfranchised terrestrial radio employees and some visionary venture capitalists. They know that the medium they loved no longer exists. They are using their combined knowledge to rebuild it and then utilize state-of-the-art technology to deliver it. More and more subscribers are signing up every day. They are more than willing to spend the few dollars a week to receive over 100 channels of "real" radio.

It's a slow growth curve at the moment, but any one who has listened knows that they are reviving the true spirit of radio. So far, terrestrial radio has done very little to compete with the new services. There is a half-hearted terrestrial radio technology called

Hybrid Digital, or HD, (sometimes referred to as High Definition) radio, but I still don't totally understand it and I'm a radio geek. Combine that with the fact that HD radio receivers cost $300 and you have a recipe for failure.

As a salesperson, one of the most important things I've learned from satellite radio is that there's always a way to do things right. It's rarely easy, but it can be done if you look for and work hard enough to achieve your goal.

Art Glass/Smart Glass

In the early days of QVC, which started broadcasting in late 1986, many name brand vendors were leery of selling their goods on television. Most were afraid it would disrupt their existing network of dealers. It was a valid concern. For most companies, their existing dealers had been their bread and butter for decades.

Enter the late (and phenomenal) Bill Fenton, then President of the Fenton Art Glass Company. When he was approached by QVC, he had the same concern about upsetting his existing dealers. But he had an idea. He proposed creating exclusive products for

QVC that would not be available at his dealers. He also requested permission to talk about his existing dealers, reminding customers that what they saw on QVC would never be available at their local dealer...and vice versa.

It worked perfectly. Fenton Art Glass went on to be one of the most popular collectible lines offered on QVC while sales at their local dealers flourished from the increased visibility. Many of the big names in the collectibles' world followed Bill Fenton's lead and began offering exclusive lines on QVC. It was a win/win scenario.

Bill Fenton is one of the finest people I have even known. His love of his customers and respect for his dealers was and is an inspiration to me. He even gave out his home phone number on the air so his customers could call him with questions and comments. I tried my best to stop him, as we were live in 70 million homes at the time, but he was a commanding presence when he wanted to be. I let him do it. He did change the number after the phone rang non-stop for a couple of days. But he immediately instituted alternative ways, including email, for his customers to reach out and connect with him.

I had the opportunity to attend many Fenton Art Glass conventions and gatherings with him. When dealers and customers would approach him to say hello, he knew almost everyone's name. I asked him how he did it, figuring he had taken one of those memory courses. I'll never forget his answer; "These people have fed my family and employees for over six decades. They have an incredible passion for the craftsmanship of our employees. Why wouldn't I remember their names?" He also knew the names and family histories of his hundreds of employees.

Bill Fenton is a treasure. When he passed, I mourned the loss of a great friend and mentor. Every time I look at one of the beautiful pieces of Fenton Art Glass that add so much life to my home, I miss him very much. Due in large part to his positive guiding influence and the many incredible relationships he forged, his company continues to thrive.

How well do you know your customers and employees? If you know them as well as Bill Fenton knew his, your road to success just got a lot shorter.

When the Moon Hits Your Eye...

I became quite an on-air cook while at QVC. While I'll always be culinary challenged, I took enough classes to be a rather successful klutz in the kitchen. I grew to have a passion for cooking as well as cookware and cooking appliances. My cook shows were some of the most successful on the network. Like my previous story about demonstrating the guitar I designed, I didn't try to impress anyone. I made sure all my demos showed the major benefits of the products I was presenting.

Thanks to the power of television, I was often recognized in public, many times while dining at a restaurant. I've always very humbled that people who only know me through the television take the time to come up to me and say hello.

This being the case, with 20 years of TV experience, only one restaurant I've ever visited has ever taken me into the kitchen to show me what they do. Antonio's in West Chester, Pennsylvania, is a little, unassuming place, about 20 miles west of Philadelphia, that serves the best Italian food I've ever tasted.

It's all homemade, fresh and delicious.

The first time I had dinner there, Anthony, the owner, recognized me and said, "You're the guy who does all those cook shows on TV." He asked me if I ever made *pietanza da pescatore*. I surprised him when I told him that I knew it meant *meal of the fisherman* (I had a lot of Italian friends and acquaintances), and also told him I had never made it.

He took me into the kitchen and introduced me to his chef who was also his mother, Rose. She painstakingly showed me how to make the dish, even repeating parts of the recipe that I didn't understand. I couldn't wait to get on the air and show off the new recipe. Because of the different cooking times of the various types seafood it used, it was a perfect showcase for demonstrating even cooking, a hallmark of the cookware set I was demonstrating.

I also used the opportunity to thank Antonio's Restaurant on the air, telling everyone how great the food was. Already successful, Antonio's started getting calls from people all over the country who were visiting the Philadelphia area.

Since they had really helped me, I was very proud I could help their business.

I received so many requests for *pietanza da pescatore* that I not only emailed the recipe but also prepared it on-air many times. Every time, I would give Antonio's a well-deserved plug. I even took many celebrity guests there, including Ron Popeil (a very discerning diner), who loved it as much as I did. While they were already successful, I was delighted that I could add to that. Even after this, while other restaurant owners and managers recognized me as "the guy who does all those cook shows," no one ever took me into the kitchen to show me how to make a signature dish.

Do you seize every opportunity that comes your way? Are you able to recognize potential opportunities and take advantage of them? Do you often "cast your bread upon the waters" with no guarantee of success? Anthony at Antonio's Restaurant did and it got him a great deal of national TV exposure. And knowing the man quite well, I'm positive he didn't do it for gain. He is a proud restaurateur and loves to show people how his great food is prepared. I found out that he has always shown his customers how his food is prepared, even sharing proprietary recipes. His extraordinary customer service has really paid off.

By the way, I still eat there every time I'm back in the Philadelphia area. Hope I'll see you there someday!

Trade Show Savvy

For over two years, I made my living as a trade show magician. It was my job to weave the features and benefits of a company's products and services into a compelling sleight-of-hand performance. I would build a crowd and then finish with as line like, "Obviously, what you've just seen are illusions. The real magic comes from the products, systems, and services of XYZ Corporation." Yes, I was the corporate version of a Judas Goat. But it was a lot of fun and really helped my customers to generate more qualified leads.

I was always amazed by the behavior of the people who were staffing the trade show booths. Some companies had a rigorous training program. They let their people know how important these events were and had a list of guidelines for booth behavior. Most did not allow sitting, eating, or drinking while in the booth.

Their staff was told to treat everyone who entered the booth as a prospective customer. These booths were always busy and extremely successful.

It was easy to tell which companies had not trained their booth personnel. You've seen them too, probably too many times. Their people are often eating and drinking, talking to each other, ignoring people entering the booth. It's as if the trade show is a big party and potential customers were not invited. These companies might as well take all the money they spend attending the trade show and throw it down a rat hole. At least they might get a new pet.

If you do trade shows, conventions, or any other gathering where you want to get more customers, make sure that your booth personnel are properly trained. Let them know how important their role is at the particular event. Make it fun for people who enter your booth. Don't just let people have fun for fun's sake. Make sure your employees qualify all the potential customers. They know why they're there and they will respect that you are treating them like fellow professionals.

I recently went to a cable TV trade show and went into a booth that had an electronic shooting gallery. I waited in line and had a great time blasting various targets. After complimenting me on my marksmanship, a member of the booth team thanked me for coming in and gave me a goody bag full of some great "swag." No one tried to qualify me as a prospect. I wasn't even given a pep talk about the network; in fact, no one at the booth even mentioned it. By the way, I found out that the booth was promoting a cable network that is not doing very well. No surprise there.

A Whale of a Tale

This anecdote would have fit into many different chapters, but I thought it would be a great way to go out on a high note. A few years back, I had the opportunity to host a series of shows on QVC featuring the merchandise from the movie *Free Willie*. At that time, the orca Keiko (Willie's real name) was being kept in a small tank at an amusement park in Mexico City.

I was thrilled when I heard that we were going to film Keiko in Mexico. Knowing me all too well, my superiors told me that our insurance would not cover me if I decided to get into the tank and swim with the orca. They also told the producer to make sure this didn't happen.

Once we arrived at the amusement park, the crew was shocked when I approached the tank and put my hand out to summon Keiko. When he swam over to me, very cautiously I might add, I kept my hand extended, reached into his open mouth and began to scratch his tongue. The crew was shocked. Here was this middle-aged geek scratching the tongue of a 7000 pound orca...and we were both smiling.

What they didn't know was that I had spent weeks studying orcas (once you do, you hate the term "killer whale"). Along with the library and the Internet, I had also sought out the assistance of a local marine biologist to learn everything I could about Keiko's species. Among other things, I learned they love to have their tongue scratched.

The producer was so impressed by this example of "orca-human bonding" that he suggested I don a wetsuit and get in the tank with my new friend, as it would make for great TV. I had expected to do a lot of begging and pleading to get to this point. I was in the tank in minutes.

It was one of the most wonderful professional experiences of my life! The video looked great and the shows were extremely successful. The customers enjoyed watching Keiko and me swim like old friends, so much so that many of the items in the show sold out. As I'm sure you know, unlike traditional TV, success in televised shopping is measured by sales, not ratings.

If I hadn't taken the time to learn everything I could about orcas, there is a good chance that this extraordinary event would never have happened. I also paid the marine biologist for his time, realizing that the expense would never be approved for reimbursement. There was no doubt in my mind it was what I had to do to host a successful show.

QVC also got involved with the campaign to get Keiko out of the relatively small tank in Mexico and have him released into the ocean. We were among the many companies and individuals who were able to get him back into natural waters. He lived for many years, learning to live as an orca in the open sea.

I learned some very important lessons from this incident. First of all, outside of my dog Mandy, I have never felt such love and admiration for a non-human as I have for Keiko. I swam with and rode on a creature that could have swallowed me whole. But this gentle giant just wanted to play and eat salmon, a calling that I completely understand.

I also learned that even a huge corporation could do some real good in the world while it continues to thrive in the business world. We live in amazing times.

In Conclusion

Again, thank you for buying and reading this book. I hope you had a few laughs along the way while you picked up some useful techniques to take your sales to the next level.

Remember, as I said in the chapter titled "The Eternal Student," your learning should never end. The best way to stay at the top of your game is to continue to learn and practice your skills every day.

Ever wonder why Jack Nicklaus and Tiger Woods are such incredible golfers? Throughout both their careers, while their peers were partying, they have been practicing and learning. They knew what it takes to be great and they did it. They understood there is a cost to be the best in any field and they readily paid the price. Does that mean they didn't take time for fun along the way? Of course not. They just put it in perspective.

Don't stop with this book. Continue to grow, improve and always take time to enjoy your success. Don't hesitate to email me from my website, http://www.stevebryant.tv. I answer all my email and look forward to hearing from you.

May you and yours enjoy the best health, happiness, and success that life has to offer!

Index